1

PREFACE

VOICE AND VISION

Prose and free form poetry

Inspired by nature, people, and life experiences

A composition of humor, laughter, satire, dreams, prose, anecdote, paintings, and drawings

DEDICATED

To Leo Francis & Mary Honoré for passing on courage, strength, prudence, wisdom, intuitiveness, kindness

And to my family and friends

DRAWINGS AND PAINTINGS ARE ORIGINAL

FOR INFORMATION – perdmontempsms@gmail.com

CONTENTS

4

5

Part Nine: WE MUST OVERCOME 236

8

Part Ten: VOICES OF THE PEOPLE

9

1

1

1

1

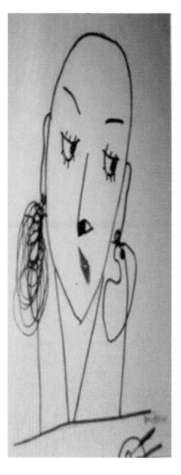

THE MUSE

Part One: The World! Through Whose Eyes?

Whose Eyes

Through
Whose
Eyes
 Do
You
See
The
 World?

Whose
Opinions
Do
You
Roll
Out?

I see
You need
To question
 more
Question
 More!

Looks

Looks
Can
Be
Deceiving

All
That
Glitters
Is
Not
 Gold

That
Statue
You
See
Has
Another
Story

Loving
Eyes
Cannot
See

It's a Heavy Price for Modern Life

I see
Earth in peril
Billionaires
Joy-riding
In space
Tv and phone
Disruptions
Notifications
Unwanted
Commercials
Bombarding
Your
Mission
Frustrating
Your
Life
It's a heavy
Price
For modern
Living

The World is a Stage

The
World
Is
A
Stage

People
Are
Trapped
In old
And
Set
Ways

Ill-informed
Or
Unequipped
To change
Traditions
And
Situations

Living in Illusion

Your
Comfortable
Living
Is
An
 Illusion

You
Are
Too
Afraid
 To
 Face
The
 Confusion

Get up!
Make that
Move now!
Late is
Better than never

8

A Man's World

I see
A man's world
Greed and profit
Slavery
Bondage
Unending wars
Gross inequality

Hatred
Racial terror
Fear
Oppression
Violence
Mayhem

No global
Security
Evil invisibly
Lurking
Always finding
Opportunities
Hell on earth
Is what I see

Unbalanced World

I see
An unbalanced world
Survival of the fittest
Among rich, poor
Young and, old

I see tomorrow
 No different from today
 I see countries confused
And people knowing
Not what to do
Seek comfort from the bible
To contend with a one- sided
world view

I see women
 In boardrooms
And young girls and boys
Fighting wars
In the front line

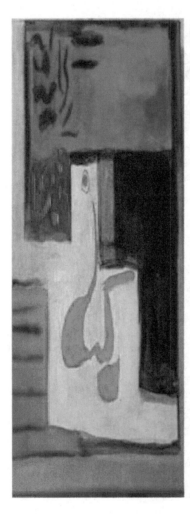

Leaders and Big News

I see
 leaders talking
As if in defense
Not to offend
Preaching
To the
Converted
Instead of
 Informing
The masses

Big news
Featured
At the dead
Of night
When
The masses
Are asleep
Drank too much
Or too tired
To think

Stokely's Mission Versus Modernization

I see
 Stokely Carmichael's
Mission
Compromised
By infomercials
Black and beautiful
Has gone out
Of the equation

A new packaging
Is on the front line
Supporting
 A multimillion billion
Skin-whitening
Cream line

I see
Modernization
Without education
Is an extremely
Dangerous situation
Plaguing nations

No Mercy

I see tent city
In Arizona desert
Baby jail
 In Houston Texas
Zero tolerance
Of Donald Trump
 Administration
For asylum seekers

I see
Criminalization
Of migrants
Children separated
From parents
Held in wire
 And chain linked
Cages

I see no mercy
Just racism
Stupidity
Or poor policy

Pursuit of Peace

I see
 Pursuit of peace
Difficult to reach
Live and let live
Is the way
 It should go
Yet
Cooperation
 Is hard
To flow

Do not block
 My driveway
I do not want
 Your squash
Growing
 On my fence
I do not like
 The way
You dress
 Yourself
Or braid

Your hair

I do not like you
As my neighbor
I do not want
To hear your preaching
On your bullhorn
I have my own religion

I do not like you
Selling water
Bird watching
 BBQing
In this public park
I will call the police
I am sure they will
Find you wrong
Because you're black

I see
Angry people
Without moral
 Integrity
And devoid
Of humanity

Color Line

I see
Color line
Blurred
If riches
Abound
If genius
Is found

I see
Modernization
Without
Education
Is an
Extremely
Dangerous
 Situation

A Man's World

I see
A man's world
In super decadence
No global security

Hatred
Racial terror
Greed
Profit
Slavery
 Bondage
Gross
 Inequality
Hell on earth
Is all I see

I see black women
Climbing to success
Amidst racism
And bullets
 Through
Their windows

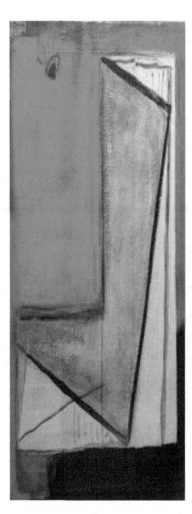

Bionic Revolution

I see
A bionic revolution
With a superhuman
In a digital evolution
Emerging in nations

A microchip
In the brain
Will differentiate
Bionic versus
Real humans

Robot and algorithm
Moving humans
To the unknown
And peace prize
Given
Before peace
It Is won

The Black Effect

I see
 Black ils the night
Without light
Powerful
And mysterious

Black
 Has its effect
 On white
Chemical
Reaction
Human
Confusion

Mark of
Identification
Used
By haters
And racists
Predators

Patriarchal Decadence

I see
Patriarchy
 Afraid
Of women
Tighten
Political
And Economic
Reins

I see patriarchy's
Train
Crashing
And women
 Waiting
To occupy
 The drivers
 Seat

Could be
 Minutes
Or a lifetime

Renaissance for the Soul

I see
A revolution
Looming
Towards
A new world
In operation
People moving
For a new vision

A new
Conscience
A renaissance
For the soul
A new view
Of humanity
New political
Ideology

New religious
Philosophy
Truth
To be set free
Light to shine
On all humanity

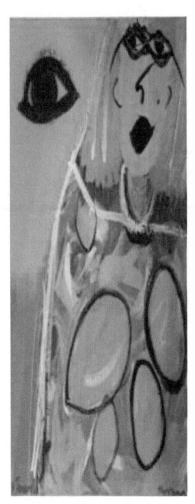

The Jury is Still Out

I see
Women
Brainwashed
With
False
Information
Reluctant
To free
Themselves
From
Patriotic
Domination
To fix
Their
Situations

Anyway!
The jury
Is still out

23

Part Two: Life is a Precious Opportunity

Sleeping Beauty

Life does not end
It changes
For better
 Or worse
With
Or without
Purpose

Some things in life
Are inevitable
One thing is certain
There is choice
 Life is like that

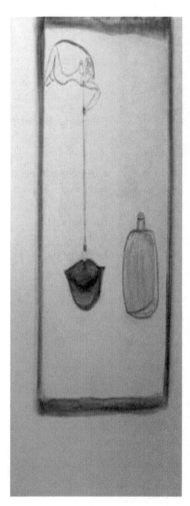

Honey Milk

Life does not end
 It Changes
Change
 Is inevitable
Revise perception
Control situations

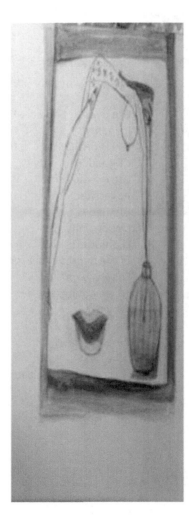

Energy in a Bottle

Life does not end
From birth
To death
 It changes

It is like that

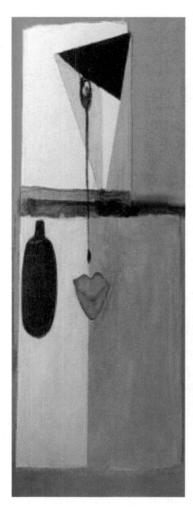

Black Tears

Life does not end
It changes
Life is duality
Of good, bad, ugly
Life encounters
Adversity
Life needs
Opportunity
Life flutters
In the depths of reason
For answers
To why things happen
Why this
Why that
Why me
Why not
No comprehensible logic
For this or that

Positivity

Always look
On the bright side
 Of things
Hope for light
At the end of the tunnel

Ferdinand

Change
The
 Reality
Of
 Your
Thinking
Question more
Who
What
When
Where
Why

Read My Lips

You are not
 Hearing
 My words
Read
My sips!

Don't Worry

Don't worry
Think how
To solve it
List options
Do first
 The most likely
If it fails
Try the next
Then the next
Try the next
Try and try again
You will succeed
 At last
Use supreme
Mind control
It may seem
 Impossible
Until it is done

The Web Around You

Friends may
Bring you go
They may not
 Bring you back
Their love
May be a trap

They can spin
Webs around you
Time will come
When you must
 Break free

Inner Self

Listen to your
Inner voice
Let your
 Conscience
Be your guide

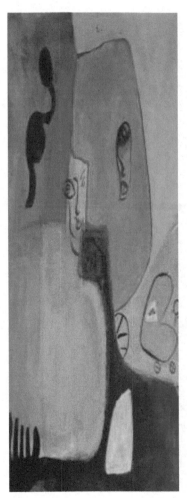

Will and Way

There is will
Anywhere
There is a way
There is will

Ups and Downs

Life has its
 Ups and downs
Perseverance
Is the crown

36

Opportunity

A Little window
 Of opportunity
Is better than
 Nothing

Serendipity

Nothing happens
By chance
Coincidences
Are the workings
Of a higher power

Every
Disappointment
Is a blessing

One must develop
A weapon
Against adversity

Monkey knows
Which trees to climb

"The seeds of fear
Once they are sewn
Begin to grow in your
Imagination"

38

You never miss

The water
 Till the well runs dry

Look for the wisdom
In everything

Always get
 The background
To fully understand
 The picture

You reap what you sew

Too many cooks
Spoil the broth

Do the math
 Reconciliation
+ Healing = peace

They can do it
If they want
They cannot do it
 Forever

Prevention
 Is better than cure

Do you have a dog?
In the fight

You live to learn

How you make
 Your bed
 So, you shall lie

 It takes two
 To make a quarrel

Two wrongs
 Do not make right

Do not trouble
Trouble
Unless trouble
Troubles
You

You cannot fight
 fire with fire

What goes up?
Must come down

Think twice before
you make that move

Smoke always finds
A way out

Where there is smoke
 There is fire

Do not bite
More than you can
 Chew

Do not burn
 Bridges
 After you cross them

Do not count
Your chickens
Before
They are hatched

A set- back
Is a set up
For a comeback

Drunk or sober
Mind your business

New broom
Sweeps clean
Old broom
Knows the corners

A promise
Is comfort for a fool

Sill waters run deep

"Everything
Has its limit"

If you have
Glass windows
Don't throw
Stones

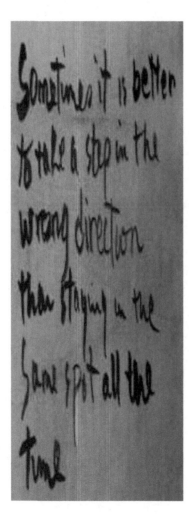

Sometimes
Monkey
Do all the work
Baboon chop
All the benefits

Don't be afraid
To make that move
The journey
 Begins
 With the first step
It always seems
Impossible
Until it is done

Sometimes
 It takes
A step back
To make
 A comeback

Bad Mistake

Higher Power laws

Change does not exist
There are laws
 Of coincidences
The workings
 Of a higher power

Life is Like a Butterfly

A beautiful, wise
 Brave butterfly
 Lived In a fountain
It played a little game
If someone tried
 To catch it

Each time
 Narrowly escaping
It perched on a fence
 And stared at them
Thinking

You want to rob me
Of my life and liberty
You just want me
For my beauty
For a moment of pleasure
For a trophy
For selfish desire
Life is like that

Life is Like Snowflakes

Life can be soft
And gentle
Like snowflakes
It can hit
 like a blizzard
When times
 Are hard
It is like a river
 Flowing gently
Weaker
And weaker
 Forever

Life is an Act

Life is an act
The world
 Is the stage
Road rage
 On highways
Peace marches
Protests in parks
If you agreed to
 Or not
You are in the acts
Afraid to speak
Watching
 Whose directing
Operating
Deciding
 your fate

Life is Like That

It is
What it is

Loud Talking
Public
 Information
Opinion?
 Is it everybody's?
 Business?

Say What?

Good and Bad

It is two strands
Of your hair
Pulling
 Against each other
Good and bad
Is inherent
 In all things

Cosmic Mission

Choose an opinion
That will liberate you
If even it is the
Inconvenient truth

Rise

Rise
 To your higher
 Understanding

Cosmic Mother

Do not be stuck
On the lies you've taught
That you fail
To see the truth

Reciprocity

Every good turn
Deserves another

The Artist

life
Without
Imagination?

You can
Always
Tell an artist
When you
 See one

Art makes
The world
Go around

Window
Of
Opportunity

Strike

Strike
 While the iron
 Is hot
 Girls
Delay can be
Dangerous

60

Destroy Earth

You will find heaven
And moon
A better place
To grow your vegetables
Yes?

Part Three: BLUES

62

Blues or Jazz
Blues

Blues

Blues is all we have

If you cannot
Find happiness
Life will be nothing
But the blues

All
 You
  Play
  is blues

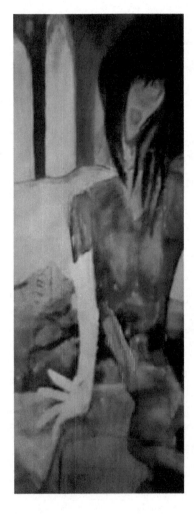

She has blues
To remember
Forever
Reckless moments blues

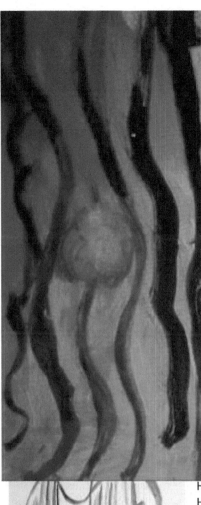

All the World has

Is Blues

Blues in the morning
Blues at the night
Blues when the rent's due
When the sky is blue
When the sun shines
When there's crime
Rich people blues
Poor people blues
Lottery blues

Gun control blues
Funky blues
Fake news blues
Bombs and wars blues
Terrorist blues
Homeless blues
Hunger blues
Famine blues
Refugee blues
Freedom and justice
Blues

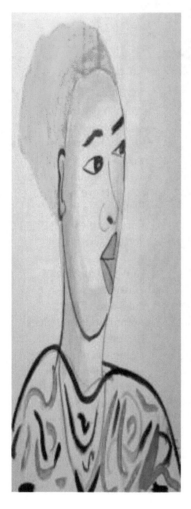

Oppression blues
Lonesome blues
Lonely heart blues
Economic blues
Hardship blues
Nine to five blues
Pay day blues
White woman blues
Black women blues
Black Lives Matter
Blues
Asians matter blues

Sugar mama blues
Baby mama blues
Mother-in-law blues
Devil got my woman
Blues
The devil made me
Do it blues
Lover man blues
Kindhearted woman blues
Cheating-man blues
Baby daddy blues
Husband snatcher blues
Broken heart blues

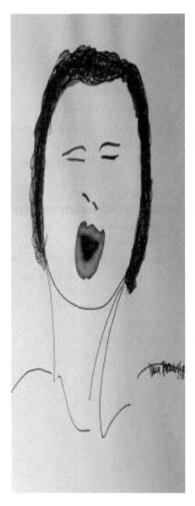

Black capitalism blues
Sexism in academia blues
Republican blues
Immigration blues
Refugee blues
Democrat blues
Voting rights blues
Trump white house
Blues
George bush blues
Hilary blues
Obama blues
Markel blues

Russian blues
Belarus blues
Paris blues
London blues
New York blues
African blues
Latin American blues
Third world country
Blues
Joe and Kamala
 Sing the blues

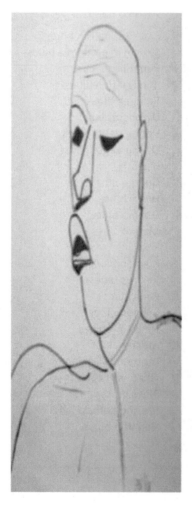

Middle East blues
Afghanistan women and girls
Have blues to remember
Palestinians sing the blues
Palestinians have
 Blues to remember
Blues in the Korean
 Peninsula
Freedom blues
Activists journalist get the blues
All the way to eternity blues
Wall Street blues
World Bank and IMF
 Blues
Hip hop blues

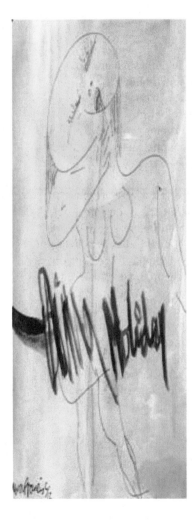

Billy Sings
The Blues

My iceman
 Is a good man
Just as nice
 As he can be
My woodman
 Is a good man
Cause he likes
 To keep me warm
 When his wood
Don't burn
 To suit me
 He takes me
 In his arms

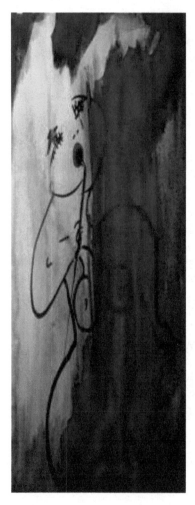

They put a spell on you
Brainwashing
Is a spell on you
Decolonize
Your mind
Break the spell
They cast on you

They put a spell on you
Media cast a spell on you
Capitalism has a spell on you
Mc Donald's has a spell on you
Fast food has a spell on you
Break the spell
They cast on you

They put a spell on you
Computer has a spell on you
Leave your room
Wash your eyes
Remove the spell on you
They put a spell on you

We've got blues
Blues to remember
Blues
Blues all over
The world

BB and Lucille

Breaking News

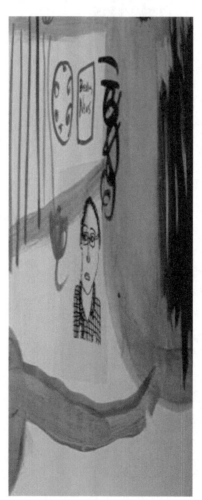

Where to?

Take
The
    A
  Train

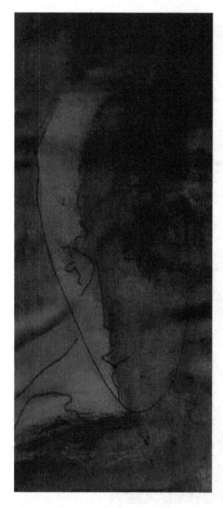

Part Four: FACTORS

Money
Time
Dream
Night
Day

Money

Money makes
loud noises
Vain soul rejoices
Hearts
Wither from greed

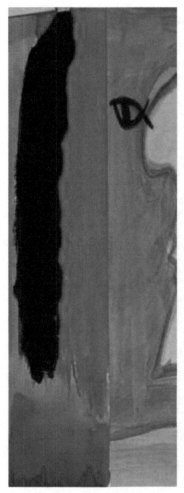

Time

Time is illusion
Time has no color
 Sound or form
Yet, so profound

Time is infinite
Definite
Precious
It waits for no one

You cannot hold on
 To time
It is not like money
 It is like money
A priceless
Precious
Commodity

Night

Mystery night!
I am no longer
Overwhelmed
With delusions
Of your peacefulness
What is peace?
A dog barking
Continuous
A baby crying
its mother
Lamenting
Her misery
A tree full of birds
Twittering all night
Mosquitos
Feasting on
Unprotected
Bodies

Your blackness
 Sooths me
The stars
 The moon
Give me joy
Breathtaking joy
Knowing
There is light
To sooth
 Your mystery

The night guard's
Absolutions
Nagged at my head
And as I attempted
 To grasp the sleep
 That seemed
 So near
A rooster crowed
I wished
 How I wished
For your
Peacefulness

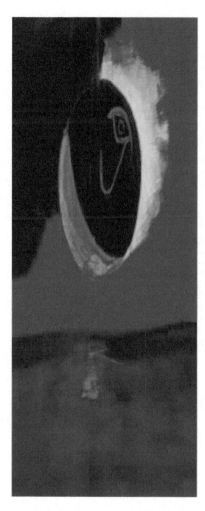

Last Night

Was last night
Restless
Mysterious
Delirious
Sublime
Divine
Or all dreams?

Somewhere Last Night

Somewhere
 Last night
People
 Shut their eyes
Some could not sleep
Or catch a wink
Some as restless
 As could be
Filled with fear
That they may
Have to flee

Fear restlessness
Crept In the darkness
People lay awake
Wondering
If they should run
A difficult decision
When life is at stake
 And chance of survival
 Slim

Tonight

Tonight
Many people
Do not want
To be in darkness
But they are
Because
Of circumstances
They cannot
Control

Today

This beautiful
 Wonderful
Amazing day
Will rejuvenate
 Its energies
Like a volcano
For tomorrow

Tomorrow

Tomorrow
Inexorable
 Tomorrow!
Some people
Will be in the cold
Not because
They want to be
In cold
But because
The world is good
And bad
Good and bad
Is the nature
Of all things

No Resting Place Among the Ginger Lilies

Around midnight
Something fell
On the roof
Perhaps a bat
Dropped a fruit
On its nightly route

A sudden hush
Engulfed the house
When the silence
Broke
A mutual feeling
Was afloat
That maybe
Sweet Mary
Returned
To protest
Not laid to rest
Among the ginger
Lilies
She loved best

Call Faith

If it is late
If darkness falls
If you cannot call
If fear appears
Hiding
In a plastic bag
Behind
A broken
 Glass window
Call faith

Peace Profound

A powerful sound
Like a rumble of thunder
Filled the air
With mayhem and fear

The earth trembled
The whole city crumbled
Hell had let loose
All its troubles

An artist and her painting
She named Peace Profound
Were pulled unscathed
From under the rubble

The artist was unsound
It was a miracle nothing
Happened to Peace
Profound

The artist's imagination
Was shattered
She drifted, wondered
In and out of reality
In New York City

At the Metropolitan

Museum
She joined Strangers
Viewing a painting
She vividly
Remembered

A painting of a naked
Pregnant woman
Optimistically waiting
To deliver the child
From her protruding belly

The viewers
For a moment
Seemed convincingly
Entranced
Until one of them
Broke the spell
When she calmly said

Peace profound
What wonderful
World it could be
If she was free

Dream Adventure 1

She did not feel the ground
 Under her feet
Or the leaves
Slapping her as they did
When she walked by

She felt only
A gentle breeze
 Caressing her
As she floated swiftly,
Smoothly

She landed at a house
Where a woman
 Was about
At the front
Tending to plants

The woman sensed
She wanted to speak
And tilted her head
 To listen

She had in mind

To ask of a man
But as she thought
Of the question
Another woman
Sitting under a shed
Caught her attention
And she ran
To her instead

That woman handed
Her a child
Then floated away
In the sky
Over a drenched
Droopy green bush
Under which muddy
Water flowed
Swiftly down
A meandering path

Dream Adventure 2

A dream
 Is an adventure
Into strange
 Experiences
To do things
Not possibly
True
To escape
Situations
And feel
 Like a champion
To look inward
And in the world
Around
In all the things
To analyze
 The wisdom
Strangely meant
For you

Dance With Urchins

The lights
Went out
The night
Was still
She woke up
From
Her mother's arms
She floated
Upward
Over
The canopied bed
And danced
With urchins
While her mother
And sister slept
She woke up
Again
It was morning
She remembered

Levitation

Standing by her bed
She watched herself
Sleeping
And felt connected
To her sleeping self
By a ray

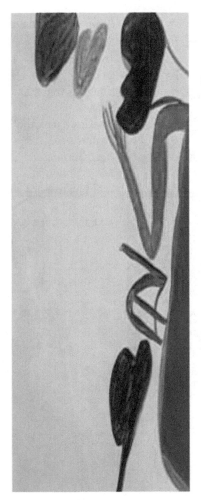

Part Five: LOVE

Fragrance of Love

The fragrance
Of love
Draws us together
Souls
 Seeking each other
To nurture
Flesh burning
Spirits unbound
Yearning to learn
The secrets
 Of each other's
 Heart

Love is Magic

Love
 Is
 Magic
Life
 Mystery
A moment
A thought
Feelings
Funky Jazz
 Blowing
African music
 Rolling
 Reggae
 Jamming
Souls
Searching
Seeking
Love
 Peace
Understanding

Love is Mystery

Love
Is
Mystery
 Motion
Like
The
 Ocean
Swelling
 Subsiding

Soul
Searching
For joy
 wisdom
truth
Spirit
 Waking
 Wanting
Freedom
Peace
Satisfaction

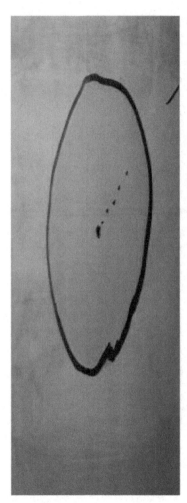

An Element of Love

A possessive
Element
Of love
Guard's love
A possessive
Element
Of love
Possesses love
True love
Possesses
Uncertain love

Yellow Tears

Love is all she had
She took her baby
 In her arms
In silence
Or in words
Come here my love!

She held it close
She watched fire
Getting closer
From
The coal inferno
She sat over
In Jakarta India

In silence
 Or in words
 Each time
 She took her baby
 In her arms
Come here
 My love!

White Tears

A mother
In despair
Dying
 Of starvation
Running from
Oppression
Showed
 Her love
Until
 The very end

Taking her baby
In her tired arms
In silence
Or in words
Come here
 My love!

Red Tears

In silence
Or in words
Come here
 My love!
A desperate mother
Wrapped her Baby
In a blanket
Hugged
Kissed
Held it tight
And cried
She Hugged
Kissed
And cried
Again, and again
She threw the baby
Out the window
Hoped someone
May catch her
A desperate mother
Caught in Britain's
Grenfell tower
Inferno

Black Tears

Her countenance
 Changed
As she recalled
One could feel
 Her pain
She did not pause
To wipe sweat
And tears
 Streaming
Down her face
And in the soup
She stirred

Stirred
 As if she
Wished to crush
Things that came
Unawares
In her life
And took her joys
And her children
Leaving her
Defenseless
Leaving her
 In pain

A Child is a Child
Anywhere
In the World

Refugee children
From
Central America
Suffer the wrought
Of immigration
In detention camps
At the border

Taken from
Their parents
Crying
Freezing
Dirty ill faces
Wrapped in foil
Sleep on mats
On concrete floors
In jammed in cages

A Child is a Child
Anywhere
In the World

100 children
And their mothers
Hoping
For freedom
And peace
Traveled
 From Idlim
To Rashadeeme
 Warring rebels
 Gave them sweets
Before
 Blowing them
To pieces

A Child is a Child
Anywhere
 In the World

Two million
 Innocent children
Caught up
 In ruthless wars
As human shield
 For rebels
And collateral
 For allies

In Yemen
19 million needs
 Humanitarian help
From cholera
And diphtheria
7 million
 Starving to death
 From drought
 And famine

One child died
In flint Michigan
Twenty-two
 Children died
 In Manchester
 England
 Whether in Paris
Germany
Australia
Yemen
 Syria

Venezuela
 South Sudan
 Pakistan
 Northern Uganda
 Palestine
Nigeria
 Saudi Arabia
Afghanistan
 Or America

A child is a child
Anywhere
 In the world

A little boy saw
His parents killed
In front of him
A little boy
Lost all his limbs
And forced
To sing
In a make- shift
School

A little boy
Lost his friends
And his country
In wars
Ran for his life

Lost in towns
Tired
Sick
Missing
Home
And parents
Love

A Child is a Child
Anywhere
In the World

Little boys
Drafted
As soldiers
Returned from
The front line
Trying to forget
 Crimes
They saw
Or forced
 To do
With AK4's
Heavier than
Themselves

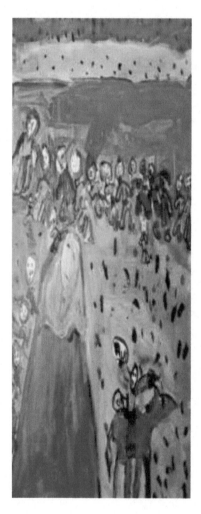

Refugee children
Flee bombs
And rebels
Nowhere
To hide
Ran
For their lives
Lost parents
Or left them dead
Under rubble

Refugee children
Go missing
In human
Trafficking
3 million
Not in schools
Thousands die
Unnoticed
A child is a child
Anywhere
In the world

Refugee boys
Unaccompanied
Minors
 At Calais
Jungle port
Jump off a cliff
To stowaway
 On a boat
Or crawl
 Under a truck
To risk
 A perilous
 Journey
Hoping
 To find safety
And asylum
In Brittany
Or Germany
A child is a child
Anywhere
 In the world

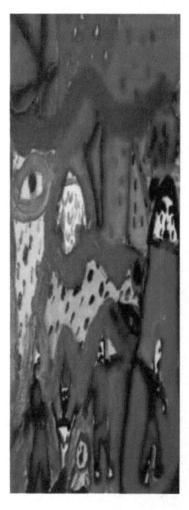

Little children
Called
Street children
Live wild
In city slums
Begging for
Crumbs
What
Circumstances
Set
A precious child
Wild
Why humanity
Leave them
Behind
Why is the world
Too busy
Or too immune
To care
A child is a child
Anywhere
In the world

Chibouk
Suddenly
Appeared In news
100 school-girls
 Kidnapped
Many months
 Passed
After

Negotiations
Between
Government
 And Boko-Haram
 Rebels
A few girls
Returned
Traded
For some rebels
Freedoms
A child is a child
Anywhere
 In the world

I am Kabuli Okara
An albino girl
Forced to live
In a refugee camp
Because of my skin
Color

I dreamed
For justice
I dreamed
To be free
In an enlightened
Society
Where people
Could see
I am not a magic
Mystery
I am as human
As human can be
I am
Mother Nature's
Creativity

A child is a child
Anywhere
In the world

Hundreds like me
Live hiding
From the sun
And running
From headhunters
And witch doctors
That want albino
Body parts
To make magic
For riches

I watched in court
The men
That took my arm
I forgave them
For their ignorance
I knew the curse
Of capitalism
Drove them
To the heartless
Deed

I know education
Is the answer
To a superstitious
 Ideological disaster
Driven to extreme
By false education
 And economic
 Deprivation
I want the world
 To be informed
To liberate minds
And change
 Opinions
For a better
 Humankind

A child is a child
Anywhere
 In the world

A Mother's Lamentation

One day
 You have a child
Next day
 It is taken from you
Weeks later
They found his body
In an alley

The police
 Have no leads
Who is responsible?
No child to kiss
 And cuddle
No child
 To go home to
The police
Have no clue
What happened?
To your boo
A child is a child
Anywhere
 In the world

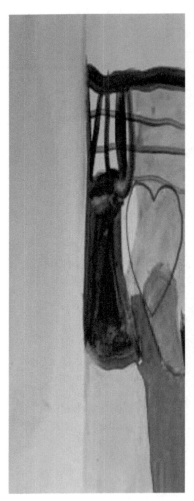

Love and Discipline

Honeybunch
Sugar dumpling
Sweetie pie
Dodo darling
Climb the tree
Pick nutmegs
For mommy

This stone is hot
Let me spit on it
Go! Hurry!
Come back quick!
Before my spit dries

Love Defies Death's Custom

Should I
Not love him
For my love
He defied
Death's custom
As soul
Sought soul
For life
Spirit
Transmigrated
Spirit gain
Sprit lost

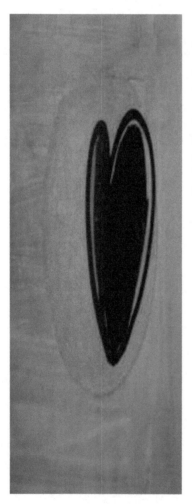

No Passion

To have no passion
Then you have not
 Discovered yourself
Where love
Cannot dwell
Or peace repose
Tormented soul
Seek thyself

Without Love and Compassion

Love escapes
The heart
In this
 Decadent
 World
Sorrows
Are laughter
Brother
 kills brother
Color hates color
Make no sense
Whatsoever

Peace Reconciliation

Peace
Reconciliation
Is a great vision
To restore
Conditions
Where love died
Or gone to hide

I love You More

I love you more
If even
You do not hear
From me
If you
Misunderstood
Misjudged
Hated
Or hurt me
I still love you

I love you
Because
I understand
In fact!
I love you more
If you love me
At all

It is Time

To Change the
Beat

Instead of
 Reckless
Smears
Secrets
 Lies
Plotting
 Strategizing
Demonizing
Delegitimizing
Masterminding
Misrepresenting

Destroying
Complaining
Condemning
 Making
 No effective
Negotiations
 For solutions
Spying
Killing

Attacking

Counter
 Attacking
Extremist's
 Attacking
Governments
 Fighting back
People
Heartlessly
Killing
 Each other

Leaders
Recklessly
Talking
 Of trigger
Finger on the
Nuclear

It is time
To change the
Beat
Love is a cool
 Thing
Try it instead

Day after day
Terrified people
Flee
Missiles
Snipers
Rebels
Weapons shot
From all sides
Bombs falling
From the sky
Urban warfare
Street by street
House by house

No
Consideration
For children
Innocent people
Babies
Orphans
Pregnant women
Old
Young
Feeble
Disabled
No one speared

Anarchy

And barbarism
Unleashed
No place to hide
From vicious
Fighting
Only death
 In sight

Nightmares
 Pain
 Sorrow
Destruction
Thousands
Dead
The wounded
 left in
Desperation

It is time
To change the
Beat
Love is a cool
 Thing
 Try it instead

Adding insult

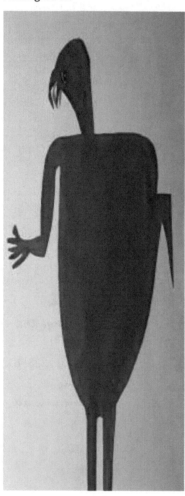

To injury
Men rescued
 From the rubble
Stripped down
 To their underwear
Lost their dignity
To prove
They carried
 No suicide vests
Or they are not
The enemy

No worry
For the players
In the game
 Of human misery

War is a game
The players feel
 No shame
Destruction
 Is the name
Of the game

Some players
Claimed
They bombed
With Bombs
That knows
Exactly
Where to hit
That innocent
People killed
Are the rebels
Fault
Or simply
Collateral

It is time
To change
The beat
Love is a
Cool thing
Try it instead

Innocent people
Lost their freedoms

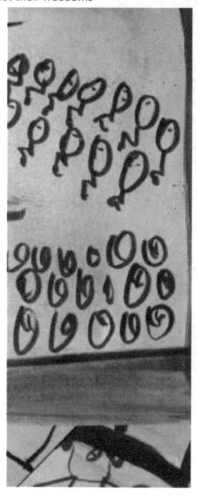

Rebels took them captive
As shield in the fight
Trapped them for days
Without food, medicine
Or water

War is a game
The players feel no shame
Destruction is the name
Of the game

Bombs falling
On the homeland
Send people fleeing
By millions
Across the Mediterranean
Thousands died
In the Greek Sea
More and more drowned
More of them tried
Heading to an unknown
Destiny

134

Heading for Italy
Many ended up
In Calais refugee jungle
Many ended up
In Australian or Israel
Penitentiaries

People had identity
They had names
They had families
They nurtured dreams
Before they were forced
To flee
Before they drowned
In the sea
Washed up on the Shores
Of Italy
And buried as numbers
In Lesbos symmetry

It is time
To change the beat
Love is a cool thing
Try it instead

Many were rescued
 Conscious and Unconscious
And wrapped in plastic
Before interrogated
For signs of terrorism

Fleeing to Europe
From terror at home
Some met more horror
Doors slammed
In their Faces
Routes closed
On their way
And fences
To keep them out
 Went up with signs
 That said
You're not welcome
Here
It is time

To change the beat

Love is a cool thing

Try it Instead

An angry Poll
 Kicked a little

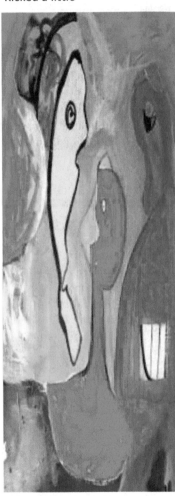

Refugee girl
Trying to cross
The polish Border

The poor dame
 Could not bear
The sight of refugees
She lost her moral
 Compass

Instead of showing
Compassion
 She kicked a child
When the child
Was down

What would you do?
Where would you run?
If your world
Came tumbling down?
Love
 Is a cool thing
 Try it instead

137

Refugees

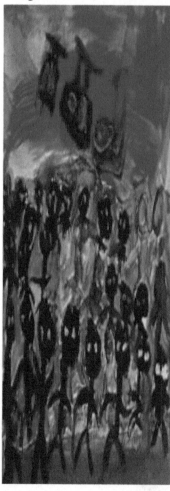

Or economic
Migrant
Call them
What you like
Some run from
Rich countries
In which corporations
Are stealing their wealth
And leaving them
In poverty

Refugees flee
Wars
Oppression
Famine
Destruction
Or inhuman
Conditions
To look for better
Safer life
As any sane human
Would
In such situation

Bombs falling
On the homeland

Send brown-skin people
Fleeing by millions

Trying to reach Germany
 They faced death
In the Mediterranean
Or trapped in Calais jungle

War is a game
The players feel no shame
Destruction is the name
Of the game

It is time
To change the beat
Love is a cool thing
 Try it instead

Black smoke rose
Refugee camp on fire
93 tents burnt down
3 left standing
100 refugee families
 Lost all
 Their belongings
Documents
 Obliterated
New problems
Generated
Trillions spent
 Building fences
 To keep them out
Where?
Can they run?
If it happened
 To you
Where?
 Would you run?

It is time

To change

Your beat

Love is a cool thing

Try it Instead

Ode To Maurice Bishop

The land looks
 Fresh and green
Where your body
May be buried
If your memory
Is in their hearts
They are not talking

Ode To Sarah Thiero

She had
 The kindest heart
The softest voice
A good friend
Is hard to find

Ode To Genevieve Ekiete

Her anguish grew
Into restless nights
Troubled days
Broken promises
Untrue friends
In a world
Too imperfect

Ode To Cynthia Honoré

Her voice echoed
She sung
Wonderfully
Each time
 She ran an errand
Caressing leaves
 And flowers
On the side
 Of the road
To and from
Wherever she went
Until her life
Joined the echoes
Of her songs

Ode To Bala Mohammed

Lenin
Stalin
Engels and
Max
Castro
 And Kaddafi
Influenced
His destiny

Ode To George Gabriel

Cousin
George
Smart
Humorous
Intelligent
Friendship
Understanding

146

Leo and Marry Sweet home

Leo was a tall
Handsome
Brown eyed
Brown skin man
Some described
Him
As a quite
Nice man
He met marry
On a bus
Said to her
I like you
She answered
I have a father

Mary
Was beautiful
As a dark red rose
Her father like the
Thons and thistles
Of the rosebush

When they married
It was good show
A breath-taking
Opportunity
For the community

Leo left
As migrant labor
To Cuba
Seeking
Opportunity
To make life
Better
For his family

He returned
Months later
Somewhat
In a stupor
Mary watched him
In despair
He watched
His beautiful wife
Holding in his hand
A handful of grass
For the mule
And horse

Suddenly
Leo passed
His life snatched
Like a fish
 From a pond
Leaving Mary
Sweet home
Sad and alone

She bore
 The pain
Never
 Complained
She refused
To surrender
To adversity
Because
 A woman
 Must do
What a woman
 Must do
She minded
 Her business
And her children

Yanit

Pinky, Yanit, and Mary
Were neighbors
Of a special kind
Mary kept to herself
Most times
Pinky had her ways
She did not speak to Mary
For reasons she alone knew
Yanit was caught
Between the two

Yanit was quite peculiar
She visited Mary
But stopped by the fence
Where Pinky could not see

She brought news
Mary would not otherwise know
Her favorite line
To Mary's reply, was always,
You don't say!

Yanit eyed the breadfruits
Hanging from the tree
Above her head
Often, the sole objects
Of her visit

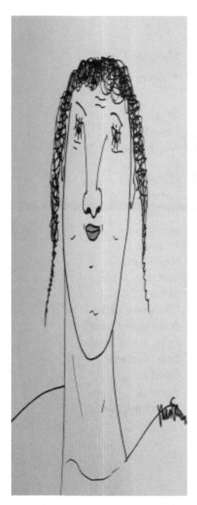

Pinky

Pinky painted her face
With white paint, one day
And looking down at Mary
Sitting at her front door
She paced the road
Back and forth

Mary Sweet home remained
Calm and composed
She knew Pinky was looking
For some trouble
She sent her children hiding
To avoid them laughing
Vowed to keep quiet
No matter what
Pinky conspired

Mary held strong opinions
About peace and quiet
She said it took two
To make a quarrel
And you could not fight fire
With fire

Museum Under
A Four-Poster Bed

Grip
Top hat
Walking cane
Horseshoe
Horse reigns
Saddle
Trowel
Level
T Square
Stone hammer
Nutmegs
Mace
Cinnamon sticks
Dried sweet root
Dried cocoa beans
Dried Cloves
Dried ginger root
Bay leaf
 Lemmon grass

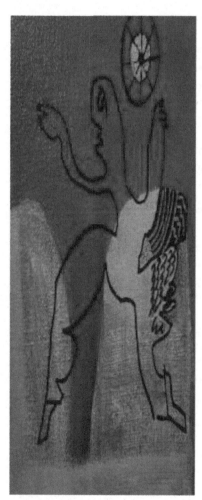

Memories

Mother's unusual love
Portrait of father
Created
 From what
 Was said of him
Dogs that knew
Boundaries
Sounds that echoed
Across green valleys
Nostalgic smells
Unfinished chapters
Of people
Places
And events

Natures Signs

When an owl hooted
Over her house
At night
She shouted
Go the poor house!

She knew
The bird brought news
Of someone
About to die

If a spider spun a thread
Down over her bed
She knew
Money would come
But knew not when

If dogs made a riot
In her yard at night
She peeped
From her window
Hoping she might see
If trouble
Was prowling free

154

Obeah Woman

Obeah woman
Your mystery
Excites me
Toss cola nuts
Tell me!
What do you see?

Barks and leaves
Veti – vert, nettle
Gru gru, carambola
Tous les mois
Divi - divi, maruba
Black sage
 bom vier
Brew in your kettle

Obeah woman!
Interpret my dreams!
Stop
 My procrastinations!
Strengthen
 My determination
 And my miss**ion!**

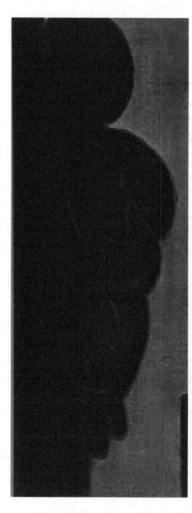

Hail Mary
Full of grace
Isis, Nut, Hathor
And Wajet
Witness
Your omens

Faded faintly
Roses
 Hangs on the wall
Saints' grotto
Spirit's grove
Affecting
 Possessing

Goat's blood
Raw eggs
Wild honey
Twenty- one herbs
Obeah woman!
Toss cola nuts!
Tell me
 What do you see?
Give me the magic
To stare my destiny

Dark Brown Cocoa

A big muscled man
 Rolled his trouser legs
Above his knees
And his shirt sleeves
Up his arms
Exposing his biceps
He looked at a caldron
Full of slimy cocoa beans
He looked at the woman
About to climb in

Her skirt was pulled up
 And secured at her waist
 With her colorful head-tie
Exposing her big
Strong thighs

She had Joyful eyes
And laughter
 That echoed miles away
She climbed with the man
In the iron caldron
And danced
 The cocoa-bean dance

Right leg up
Left leg down
Up down
 Up down
Bodies twisting
Slipping
Sliding
Giggling
Sweating
Over sweated
 Cocoa beans
Rubbing together
And separating
Sticky, slippery
Creamy
Cocoa beans
For firmness
And one
 Dark brown

158

Noble Ancestors

Noble ancestors!
I adore
Your great wisdom
Pity me!
Trapped
 In a different time
Of satires
Mad purposeless
 Games
And endless turmoil

Your blood
Was a sacred current
Life to the fecund
Earth
Our blood is spilled
For vanity
And ceaseless lusts
Noble ancestors
Avail!

Fidel the Rebel

Fought 60 years
Resisting
Western
Colonizers
Along with
Hugo Chavez
Maurice Bishop
 Che Guevara
Nelson Mandela
And other
 Human rights
 Champions
 He challenged
The
 Imperialists

Star in My Video

Moonlight, dark nights
Candlelight
Hibiscus, rubber tree
Lizards, mosquitoes
Fireflies, shearing space
 With you and me

 Streetlight's casting
 Shadows
 On the balcony
Lights, shadows, motion
A surreal composition
And you amazed
At my imagination
Watched me
Strangely
Trying to understand
If the moving shadows
Was the movie
 I invited you to see
Asking rhetorically
Who are you?
What are you

A Silent Call

I heard a silent call
Emanating
From inviolable statues
I heard it in melodies
 Of the wind
Blowing in the trees

I heard it
In the voices
 Of children singing
As if they were free
I heard it in rain drops
On the window
And in the sound
Of the speedboat
Slicing the water

A stormy cloud
Threatened my soul
As I crossed the Niger
In a speedboat
I had no clue
The boat was hired
 By a coast guard crew

The crew sat bemused
Nervous as I
The tall driver focused
 On the river
His gloomy eyes
 Captured the Niger
Spreading its body
As far as
The eyes could see

Although he sped
 Like a pro
I felt
The depth below
Wanting to take me
To a premature
 Destiny
Fear threatened me
But my mission
Was to unfold
 A destiny
I could not
 Foresee

Will You be Back?

Will you be back?
When it is dark
When the lights are out
When all is black
Will you be back?

Misunderstood

"Hi queen!"
"Look at the queen "
"You don't walk
You glide "
"She thinks she 's
A queen "
"Your face is like
A Benin queen"
"Your neck's like
Nefertiti's "
"Your voice
Is like whispering
Willows "
"I love your smell "
"Even the bathroom
Smells nice after
You use it "
"Who are you? "
"What are you? "
"Don't say that! "
"People will think
You are a witch "
"Do you make magic?

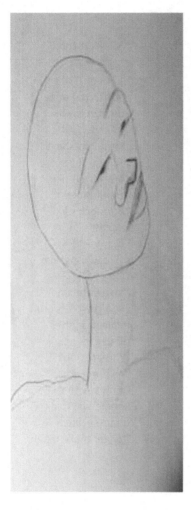

"Are you
With the revolution? "
"You look like
You could be
 A subversive "
"They think you are
 A spy "
"You look like an artist "
"Are you an artist? "
"You can always
Tell an artist
When you see one "
"You look like
 A wealthy woman "
"You should be
A rich woman "
"You behave like
 A rich woman "
"You look like
 A poor African "
"I see hatred
 In your eyes "

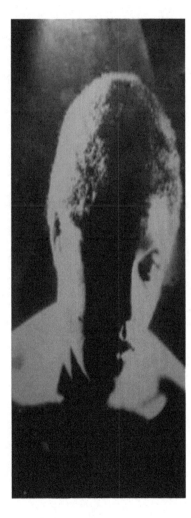

You are a snake "
"I hate you! I hate you!
I hate you!
I hate your guts! You cat! "
"You're mean, selfish
And unkind "
"But you make me feel
Good inside "
"You make me happy "
"I love you goddess "
"You are charming "
"You are a nice person "
"Women will not like you "
"Someone will discover you "
"A man will love you and leave"
"You are too darn smart "
"You talk too much "
"Do you hear yourself? "
"Women don't talk like that "
"Who are you? "
"What are you? "
"Do you talk to yourself? "
"You West Indian bitch!"

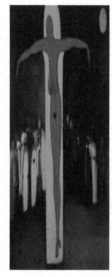

Accused

I am accused
Of
Being
Looking
Like
A
"B---h"
Witch
Magician
Spy
Revolutionary
Subversive
Artist
Wealthy woman
Poor African
Snake
Cat
Goddess
Queen
I am
What I am
And maybe
All of that

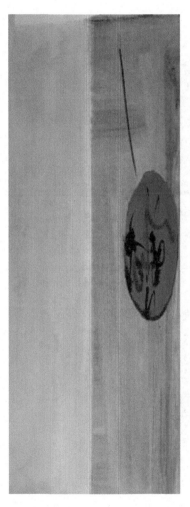

Judged by the Hole
In His Shoe

Do not judge a book
By its cover
He was a professor
With an air conditioned
Office
He was gravely
 Disappointment
At the sight
Of the small piece
 Of chicken
Sitting
 On top
 Of the rice and peas
The girl served him
She made her decision
To serve him
A small potion
Judging him
By the hole she saw
In his shoe

The Returner

He wondered alone
On the streets
That became his home
The rubbish his
 Kitchen
Tattered clothes
 And shaggy hair
Covered his body
Year after year
Is he a returner?
Destined
To walk forever?

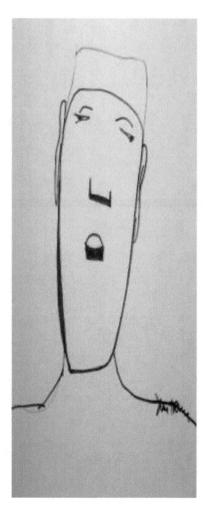

Mad?

He parked his bike
And trimmed my fence
Without my permission
Without asking
He cut the branches
Of my almond tree
To grow his yams
Was he mad?
Or simply a nice man
With a little ambition

A young boy stared
Longingly
At my guava tree
I told him to take
Instead
He pulled a plate
From his pocket
And held it out to me
I dropped in some coins
He walked away
As if that was OK

A man splashed
muddy water
On the windshield
Of the truck I sat in
He said he could not
 Destroy a business
 As poor as that

Was he a man mad?
With passion
Or a mad man
 With compassion

Another man sat
 All day in the sun
Embroidering a gown
Occasionally
He laid it down
To count coins
Dropped In his cup
By people walking by

Was he a mad man?
An artist, designer
Or a religious man
Waiting for arms
Sacrificing for Allah

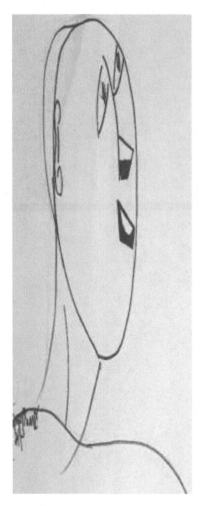

Mad Compassion?

He tore branches
Vigorously
From the almond tree
Ignoring my pleas
I could see the sun Light
Penetrating
Threatening my sanctuary
On my balcony

Without looking down
He carefully unbound
Tangled branches
 From electric wires

I shouted helplessly
Stop! Come down!
I could not reach him
Perhaps he could not
 Understand my manner
Or my foreign sound

173

Victoria....... ah!
She came running
Yes ma!
Stop him! Please!
Ma, e no understand you
I'm head no correct
Stop him please!
He is ruining my shade

Victoria clasped her hands
And curtsied for the man
Imploring him to stop
In the manner
 He chose to understand

She spoke gently
Brother! E done do oh!
E done do, well! Well!
God go bless you

The man spoke at last
Sister! Make you no vex
I break am
 So, they no go knock
 Your head
 When you waka
Around this corner

Betsy Got a Makeover

Betsy looked different
Not like any other
She wore purple hair
Several bracelets and
Finger rings
With colorful stones
Huge earrings
 In unusual designs

 Eye makeup
And lipstick added to
An amazing composition
Of dramatic colors
 Shapes and patterns
 In accessories and
Colorful clothes
 Put together
 Like a Picasso painting

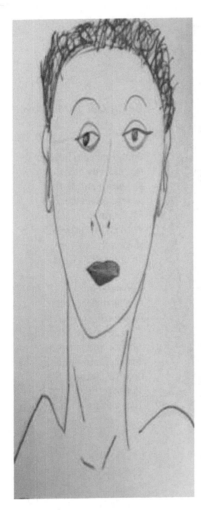

Betsy was a walking
Inspiration
People looked at her
Some with admiration
She was a work of art
For those with
Imagination

Some thought
She needed a makeover
They striped of everything
Except her bear skin
They dressed her
Like themselves

Then they clapped
And laughed
Wow! Betsy!
You look beautiful!
Betsy was silent
Betsy was gone
They stripped her
Of her Identification
Her spirit
Her imagination

Sisa Abu is a Hero

Sisa Abu Is a hero
Intelligent, strong, defiant
And quite humorous
Defending her rights
She designed
A strong husky voice
To disguise like a man
To go places
Women dared to go
To earn a living
For her family

When my husband
Was laid to rest
I was Left alone
Against the world
I want my children to live
More dignified than I have
I cry all the time
But I would eat dirt
And feed my children
Stones
Before I take
Another husband
In my home"

African Mirror

African mirror
Mammy Water blessed me
 With several children
And I screamed not once
 While in labor
See! My breasts
They are like withered
Flowers
 Day after day my skin
 Gets beaten by the weather
My face speaks of my life

My shoulders are strong
 I carry up to sixty kilos
Firewood and yams
On my head
My eyes unable to see
The road ahead of me
My hands not free
To touch my child
Tied to my back
 Another
 Stirring in my womb

I farm, I prepare soup
I feed my family
I listen to the roosters
 Melodious crows at dawn
And at sundown
I imagined how sweeter
 It the sound could be
If there was peace
In the world around me

 I watch smoke ebb
From my fire
Its embers essence
 Sooths me
I pray to see Africa free
 Of wars, exploitation
 Poverty

African mirror

I refrain from touching
Magic medicines
 I seclude my body
I purify myself
I keep my nose
Out of men's secret ways
I respect mother earth

I divined with cowries
 Instead of cola
I pledged to juju
to be faithful
To my husband
I knelt to serve him
I respected him
I made him proud
I gave him sons
 And co-wives
I whitened
 My ebony satin skin
I wore gold, Ivory
 Coral beads
Beautiful Laces
Gay-lays with messages

I mourned my husband
I shaved my head
Gave up my bed
Laid my body
On a mourning mat
I felt the earth
 Against my back
African mirror
The woman in me

I danced
 Like rippling waters
When my breasts
Were like ripe fruits
I moved my hips
Like a windstorm
To the rhythm of drums
When I sang
My voice echoed
 The life in me
Now, my eyes see
 The rising sun
But my heart, too weary
To absorb the ecstasy

I am punished, charged
With killing my husband
With hypertension
African mirror
Touch the woman in me
Only the wind
 Now caresses my body
My hopes give me strength
Courage is the comfort
For the woman in me

Woman of color
Don't Whisper Your Secrets
In the Wind

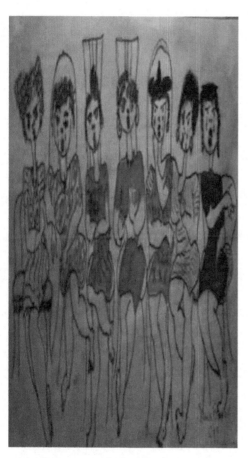

Women on Oprah's show
1989

Murder in the city 1989

Blues, Soul, Jazz
Marvin Gay
Lets' us get it on
Drown your voice
Fussing
 With your man
You drink
 Champagne
 From a
 Long-stemmed
 Glass
With a touch
 Of class
While you watch
 Evening news
Of human misery
On your big
Flat screen TV

Woman of color
Don't whisper
 your secrets
In the wind

The Nile River
Flows through
Your ancient roots
Your ancestors'
Blood
Was sanctified
For Egypt's
Ancient pyramids
Rivers, seas
Oceans
Flow eternally
In their glory

Goddess Isis
Renowned
In the ancient
World Is now
Like an eclipsed
Moon
While the mothers
Of your ancestor's
Gods
Reign supreme
You sing praises
To other
Jealous gods

Woman of color
Don't whisper
Your secrets
In the wind

Your dark skin
Glows radiantly
Shore to shore
In every nation
When the world
Was young
And pure
Virgin girls
Nurtured
Its cradle
When
Their breasts
Came out
And their hymen
Broken
Old women
Announced
A sacred door
Had opened

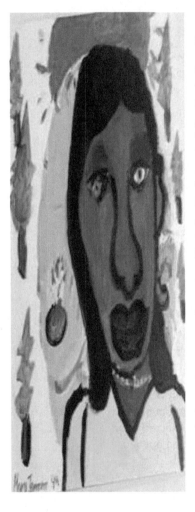

Men initiated boys
 Into manhood
Women received
Titles
For motherhood
A woman's body
Was a sacred
Temple
Men stole
Women's secrets
Defiled the goddess
And suck unborn
Babies
Out their temples

The sun goddess
 Graciously blessed
You with melanin
But when earth
 Mother
 Appels for respect
You grumble
Move to high places
To avoid children
Touching roses
Growing
On your porch

On your wall size TV
You watch more
 Children dying slowly
 In the Sahel
Where life is hell
Not a drink of water
To sooth the hunger

On city streets
Are homeless
 Mothers
Fathers
Brothers
Is it their destiny?
To walk like
 Zombies
In the land
 Of the brave
 And free

Scented candles
 Satin sheets
 A poodle with
 Manicured nails
Cuddled
 At your feet

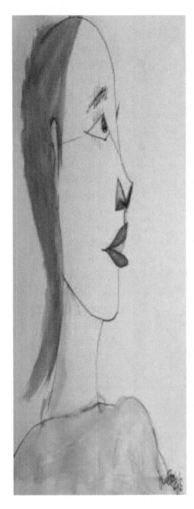

Quiet Storm
Playing
Wine chilling
You casually file
Your nails
And watch
Breaking news

Haitians
Escaping poverty
Cross the Atlantic
in dinghies
To get to Miami
Hoping to find
An opportunity

Starvation
In Ethiopia
Slavery in Sudan
War in Sierra Leon
Rebels control
The land, cut of
Children's hands
To steal
Diamonds

Is that a diamond?
On your neck
Beautiful soul sister
Sorry!
I meant!
 Beautiful diva
Does it matter?
If those *people* die
A slow, painful
 Death
 From hunger
Or a little girl's
 Hand chopped of
 For the diamonds
On her ancestors'
Lands

Woman of color
Don't whisper
Your secrets
 In the wind

191

Queen of the universe
Sunshine
Light
Darkness
Inspiration
Presence
 Without end
Habitation
Creative
Original
 Bliss
Mountain
Of Strength
Glorious
Mother
 Spirit
Sustainer
Sacred
Obscurity
 Security
Forever

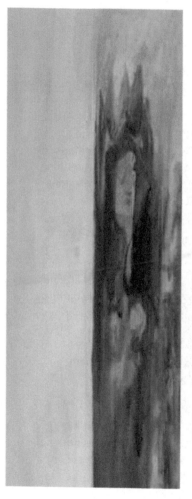

Queen of Markets

When markets
Were women's domains
Queens ruled them
Business did not begin
Until the queen
Of commerce
Sat on her golden throne

The goddess
From her temple
At the center
Of the market
Guaranteed profits

Voices echoed
Babies chuckled
People bargained
For meat and gold
When they became
Hungry
Food was always
Ready

River Ganges is Dying

River Ganges is dying
Of the waste
Dumped in her belly
As if she is nothing
Nothing deserving
Respect

Her color changes
By and by
On her surface floats
Garbage of all kinds
Still people bathe
With unwavering
Confidence
In her ability
To heal them

River Ganges
Is dying
Some treat her
As if she is nothing
Nothing deserving
Respect

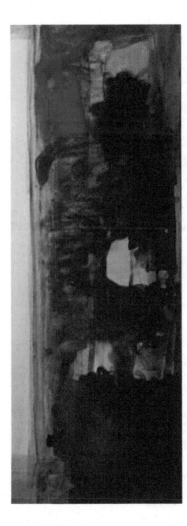

A diver
Fished a corpse
From her water
It is not
The farmer
He searches for
He drops him
And continue
Searching

The farmer
Committed
 Suicide
He could not
 Pay his debt
 To the big
Cooperation
That sold him
 The pesticides
Which ruined
His farm

River Ganges
Is dying
Greedy
Corporations
Treat her
 As if she is
 Nothing
Nothing
 Deserving
 Respect

Patron's stifle
Her with gifts
Some float
Some sink
 She can hardly
 Breathe
Clean
Or heal
She is choked up
With pollution
She remembers

She remembers
Times
 When worshipers
 Showed her
Overwhelming
 Love
Times when
 She was clean
When all kinds
 Of people
Needed
Her miracles

Times before
Industrial wastes
Heavy metal
Mercury
Started
Pouring into her
Body
Poisoning her
Killing her fishes
River Ganges

Is dying

Is Mosul Free?
A ghost town
Painful silences
Foul smell
Mass causalities
Destruction
Everywhere
Centuries
Of culture
Trampled on

Where are
The people?
Millions
Displaced
Thousands fled
Thousands
Crippled
Disfigured
Dead
Under rubble
Gone
To graveyards
No accountability
No responsibility

Is Mosul Free?

Mother's weep
Sons martyred
Tanks
Withdrawing
Chemicals
Pesticides
Hunger
Unexploded
Weapons
Are all around

Where are
The birds
Flowers
Animals
Music
Alleys
Markets
Smells
Of incense
Tea brewing
Smiling faces
With hands
Waving
Hello!

Shattered
Windows
With fearful
Emptiness
Looks down
On disfigured
Empty
Sidewalks
Empty streets
With huge
Craters
And heaps
Of rubble
In place
Of smooth
Ancient
Streets
Once bustled
With life
Where are
The people
Smiling faces
With hands
Waving
Hello!
Is Mosul free?

Is Afrin Free?

Operation
 Olive branch
 Combes around
For mines
And booby traps
My house
 Is a pile of rubble
Under which
I was buried
For days before
They pulled me out

I am alone
Without a home
My family lies
Under the rubble
I am unable
To retrieve
Their bodies
Is Afrin free?

Will Marquis Disappear
With Grandma's Bones

Marquis road is narrow
And winds gently
Along the seacoast
Its edges are eroded
And lined with trees
And small wooden
Colonial houses

The trees seemed
As if a long time ago
The wind and sea
Took the weaker of them,
And left the resilient ones
For the road and homes

The quaint little houses
With antique blue-green
Jalousies
Are fit for a museum
They struggle to hold on
As their days of glory
Slowly melts away

The grape, coconut
 And almond trees
Stands weather-beaten
Almost leafless
Especially the coconut,
 It is a symbol of endurance
Like a noble grandmother
Still struggling to protect
And nurture

Sometimes the trees
Danced the Tango
Sometimes they swayed
As happy inspiration
Sometimes as contented
 Windbreakers

Sometimes when the
Moist salty, crazy wind
From the Caribbean Sea
Blows them savagely
Their branches
Trashed each other
To the very bones
In a vicious fight
To save their lives

Clearly
 It is their destiny
They need
 A magical strategy
To protect themselves
From hurricanes,
And elements
From the beautiful
 Caribbean Sea

A little white
 Pentecostal chapel
Sat on one side
 Of the road, opposite
Grandma's house
The church converted
People of other faiths
 With singing
 And tambourine music

On Sunday's, members
 Gave greeting cards
 Too pretty to be thrown
Away
 To children to play

The church members
 Are of the opinion
Death ended life
They do not believe
In reincarnation
They buried
Grandma Bahaati
At her doorsteps
Where she dropped
 Dead, near the sea
And planted a tuff
Of wild pine trees
To mark the spot
Where she is laid

One day
Grandmas leg bones
 May wash up
On the sea-shore
 In Venezuela
And her great
 Grand children
May-be among
Curious spectators
Wondering whose bones
 They could be

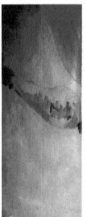

A piece of cloth
Trapped
 On a driftwood
In the spot
Where Uncle Ferdon's
House once stood
Flew gently
Like a flag
As if the sea
Installed it
To claim Marquis

When the tide broke
The water rippled
 Back and forth
Around the flag
As if to say
One day
 It will cross over
And Marquis Road
Will be no more
It will be
Under the sea

206

I walked on Marquis Road

I walked on Marquis Road
Early mornings
When the villagers
Were just stirring
Or seriously catching
Their last precious
leg of sleep

When the soothing wind
Smelt fresh like the sea
And life rippled
In the dark still
Murky, earthy, water
Under the little bridge
That separated the
Lagoon from the sea

And waxy wormy
Looking seaweeds
Bunched up on the shore
Waiting to be collected
To be sold to people
To make aphrodisiac
Mauby

I walked
 On Marquis Road
To see
 Sweet-salty sea- grapes
With dew bubbles
On their mellow skins
Waiting for children
 To suck them
Or tides to take them
 For a swim

To see sweet-salty
Purplish almonds swinging
From their branches
To tempt little children
After school bells rings

I walked
 On Marquis Road
To see uncle Fedon's
 Rows of stands
Of romaine lettuce
Growing splendidly
With the magnificent
Ocean and silvery
Horizon behind them

I walked
On Marquis Road
To see
 Along the roadside
Wild pine growing
 In large clumps
And their leaves
Cut, boiled
And bleached
Laid out to dry

And stretched, plaited
And fashioned into
 Hats, bags and mats
And decorated with huge
 Hibiscus flowers
Laid out
For tourists to buy

I walked
On Marquis Road
To watch fishermen
 Pull in their boats
Emptied their nets
And blow conk shells
To alert villagers

I walked along
The precious road
So that, I could see
 The red snapper
 Jacks, sprats
Barracudas
And flying fish
Jump around
Fruitlessly trying
To escape
 From the net

To see women and children
Some in petticoats
Swinging pretty
 Enamel bowls, running
To the fishing boats
Trying to control
The wind
Lifting their skirts
Over their bam- bam
That rolled this way
 And that
And their breasts
Dancing out of control

Ha! ha ha!
We papa!
Fish broth for dinner
Their stress-free
Laughter
Blended with
The sounds of waves
Lashing the shore
Like an orchestra

I walked
 On marquis road
Where the sights
And smells
 Of ocean and land
Aroused
 Something in me
Until one day
Uncle Ferdon's son
Fell of a mango tree
His death chilled
The beautiful things
That once
possessed me

Soubise Road

On Soubise Road
The smell of sea lime
Permeated the air
From a little
Factory
Covered with sea lime
From ground to roof
The nauseating smells
 Lingered forever
It filled the air far
Up to la Bay pair

Ruins
Of an old church
With memories
Secrets
And one stained
Glass window
Stood like a pyramid
Waiting for its fate
 To be decided

The Road to Mina

Against a glorious sunrise
Beauty In its apogee
Captivating
And mesmerizing
A huge rock stood
Like a majestic
Statue
Commanding sacrifice

At the foot
A meandering line of
Beautiful black women
With henna-stained toes
Poetic tattoos
Amazing hair styles
Jewelry, and garments
Carrying decorated
Clay pots
On their shoulders
Walked gracefully
Through a field

As the scene unfolded
Beauty, feeling
 Longing
Came together
My eyes burned
My tears rolled down
My spirit escaped
 To a place
In nature's bosom
 Where maidens sang
And children danced
And babies cried
Their first cry
Mothers sang lullabies
Around their firesides
And old women kept vigils
As virgins fulfilled
Vows of devotion
To their new husbands

A little Bus
Its Passengers
A Narrow Road

One More Looked
Like a ladybug beetle
Its windowless sides
 Gave captivating full view
Of the picturesque
Hilly countryside

Passengers sat
Shoulder to shoulder
And squeezed closer
 And closer
To make room
 For one more

A happy smile
A roll of the eyes
A low grumble, or pouted lips
Showed how someone felt
Sitting too close
 To a foe or friend

The bus traveled
The winding road
Four times a day
Carrying people
To and from
Business, work
 School and play

It turned blind corners
Tooting and hooting
Before each turn
To clear the way

It rocked and swayed
 Like a boat
On a part of the sea
Known locally
 As Kick-am-jimmy

It went up and down hills
And swerved around
Sharp bends
Giving passengers
Wicked thrills
 Or deathly scares

It stopped abruptly
Here and there
Doing free errands
Or picking up
And dropping off
Messages or passengers

The pretty little bus
Waited patiently
For anyone doing
A little run-walk
To catch it
Wiping mud of their feet
To climb it
A beauty running
And waving her hand
To stop it
Or an animal moving
To avoid it

Its engine hummed
Its radio blasted
Bob Marley sang
No Women No Cry
Some sang that refrain
With great joy

A man shouted
At the top of his voice
Turn up the volume man!
Then he sang loudly
With Bob Marley
No woman, no cry
To which a woman responded
It's a darn lie!
It's no man, no cry!
The bus rocked with laughter

It leaned left, and right
Passengers had liberty
To lean either way
Some chose quiet
Contemplation
Others went with the flow
No one showed concern
For balancing or mishap

A buxom woman
With a chaplet in hand
Seemed to pause
From praying
To adjust her wide brim
Red hat

A couple
Talking casually
 About this and that
Suddenly stopped
When the bus
Swooshed passed
A grazing donkey
After a brief contemplation
The couple resumed
Their conversation

A woman loudly exclaimed
Just hear we reach!
When she saw
An aged milestone
Barely visible in
The bush by the road

And when it swerved
To avoid hitting a cow
A crazy one leg man
Awoke from a nap
 And shouted slow
 And thoughtful
Who tie that d-- -m cow?

The bus traveled
 Where mighty waves
 Lashed the seashore
 On one side of the road
It passed picturesque
Abysses
And under giant rocks
 Poised overhead
 As if waiting
For an opportunity
To strike people dead

It glided smoothly
Down goo-goo belly road
Leaning slightly but controlled
When it dipped suddenly
A man exclaimed
"Mash the breaks man!
 For God's sake!

When finally, it arrived
At its destination
Many voices were heard
Saying
 Thank God we reach!

Drum Call

It was 4.30 am
Still as the calm
Before a storm
It came
 As if from the belly
Of the earth
It penetrated
The stillness
Appealing
To every living thing
To rise
 To face the day

Fast frenzied beats got
Louder and louder
Charged again and again
Full of new life each time
Then it subsided, softly
And soothingly

Contemplating on a Rock

Plumes of smoke
Streamed up
To meet
 A strange formation
 Of black and bluish
Fog, hanging low
In the eerie
Morning

The air smelt
 Of eucalyptus
The only sounds
Came from a tree
With branches
Spread majestically
Over a huge flattish
 Rock
Vultures lived
 In the tree
When they fluttered
The leaves fell
Like an omen

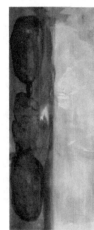

I sat alone on the rock
Contemplating
I thought about
The students police
Killed
How their cries for help
Were forever silenced

I thought about
People with power
The way they used it
About world cohesion
Food in cafeterias
And electricity

I thought
The world looked
Like what I could see
From where I sat
Under the tree
An unequal balance
Of power
Of rocks on top
Of each other
There lies the answer
I thought

Harmattan

Harmattan arrives
In cool misty mornings
With smokey grey fog
dry, cool, gloomy
And dusty
She looks like super fly
In his cream suite
And charcoal-gray hat
With his black Cadillac

Harmattan arrives
With pine wood smell
And a romantic spell
 She covers everything
With brown dust
Houses, trees, grass

She has no choice
She is hot dry trade winds
From the Sahara Desert
That blows over West Africa
From March to November

Early Morning Ecstasy

Rapture and silence
Engulfed the room
A blissful flash
Of sunlight busted in
Through screen, glass
And curtain
The rainbow it formed
On the open door
Lingered a moment
Then disappeared
Among twittering birds
In the hibiscus fence

Blue Green Rhapsody

 A willow tree
And a window
Had an amazing
 Relationship
The window had
An incredible view
The willow
 Formed the perfect
 Shade

All day, all night
The willow sighed
It seemed to cry
When the wind
 Was high

The leaves closed up
To sleep at nights
And opened up
 In the mornings
To form a magnificent
 Window awning

One morning
 For a little while
A mysterious glow
Filled the window
Willow and the window
Engaged in a tango

The wind blew the willow
Cautiously
As if not to awake
The leaves that
 Were still asleep
It blew just a flicker
In the coal pot
Of a tea vender

The teapot sat
 On the coal pot
The coal-pot
 Balanced well
On the vendor's head
He carried them
With great pride
As he served his tea
With amazing joy

The coal-pot was like a throne
For the elegant teapot
 With its long neck
Generous sprout
And spectrum of colors
Befitting its enamel status

Tea-pot and coal-pot
Were like husband and wife
Royalty, with a business
In sweet hot tea

Five days a week
The vender is on his feet
To his regular customers
All on the same street

He flipped-flopped his slippers
And jingled his cups
Just loud enough
For his customers to wake up
And dart to the spot
He laid down his pot

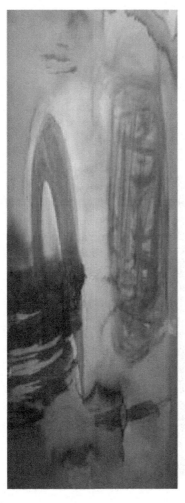

He stooped, balanced
His slim body
Tucked his white caftan
Between his legs, then
Began the tea ritual
He does so well

He set out two cups
In one he throws scoops
Of ingredients
The other he used to mix
After he added the hot tea

To mix, he fanned the tea
From cup to cup
A pleasure to see
The steam rising up
Each customer bowed
Before he sipped
One poured libation
With a poetic incantation

Each waited patiently
To get his hot cup of tea
In their favorite spot
Under the willow tree

Misty

On a beautiful day
On a quiet road
 A journey mysteriously
Unfolded
Our countenance
And sparse conversation
Showed we were worried

 We came upon a scene
Of a horrible accident
One we could not
Have imagined
Two buses, full of life
Just hours before
Laid like skeletons
Squashed tangled metal
With bits of flesh and blood
Scattered around
On the pristine roadside

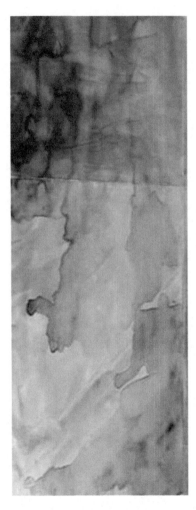

A young man
Briefcase in hand
Looked on
Entranced
We did not
Inquire
If he survived
The crash
We too were
In shock
Unable to think
Unable to use reason

We surveyed
The scene
Paused at blood
Spills
Wondered
About the bodies
That left them
We drove away
In silent contemplation

Only minutes passed
Before a grey mist
Glided out of the bushes
Across the windshield
And into the trees and fauna
On the other side
 Of the road

Simultaneously
My companions
Sadly, broke the
Fearful silence
Singing
We shall overcome

A day later
In the paper
People recalled
A mist may
Have caused
Some deadly
Accidents
On that road

Surrealism

A quiet road
No village in sight
Suddenly an old woman
 Appeared
Crossing

She held an object
To one side
Of her face
She did not pause
She looked left
Nor right

Our car
Bore down on her
We held our breath
What a miracle!
Our driver
Was magnificent
We escaped
 A horrible accident

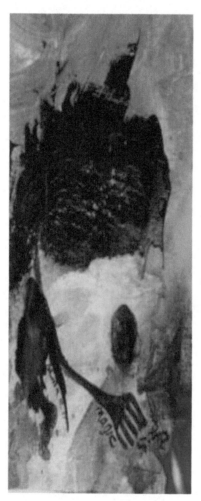

Disguised

Yellow fever
Malaria
Magic medicine
Invading water
Lilies
On Lagos marina
Swamis of locusts
In Kaduna

love portions
Gone wrong
Torrential rains
Armed robbers
Terrorists, vipers
An injection killed
A big strong man
War between
Disciples
Followers
And nations

It came disguised
As a mysterious
Poisonous gas

That oozed
 From a Cameroon
 Lake
Killing anything
It could take

It disguised
As a driver
Drove
A young woman
To post gifts
To her sister
 In America

It drove people
To work
Travelers
To Lagos
And Onitsha
It took Awolowo
In 1987
To ancestors
In heaven

It riddled six men
With bullets
On government
 Totem poles
For trafficking
Drugs
It was like sweet
 Music to which
Vista and friends
 Danced
Until dawn

It watched
Men struggled
To separate
Two Tokay-Tokay
That crashed
 Into each other

It hovered over
The passenger boy
Whose head
 Slumped
 On his chest
His mangled arm
Dangled from
The window

Unseen
It lingered
People gathered
In quiescent
Sadness
It lay-waited
A truck
That drove by
As if in flight
And another
On its back
It's four wheels
Spinning
It gave us a pass
We did not stop
We did not talk
We were
In total shock
Death
Was roaming free

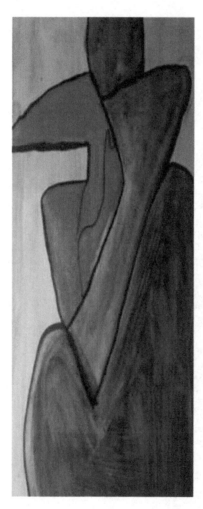

Premonition

Sweet music
Salty soup
Empty
Stomach
Pink
And orange
 Owls
Stared
From
Among
 Green
 Mushrooms
On a yellow
Canvas
 Hanging
 On the
Wall
Strange
Thoughts
Do not be afraid
Answer the phone
Hello?
 She is dead!

PART Nine: We must overcome

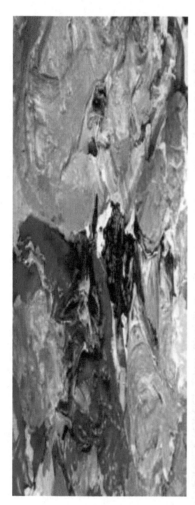

We Must Overcome Junk

We must overcome
Junk food
Junk mail
Junk noise
Junk bonds
Junk Shop
Junk plastics
Choking earth
Junk electronics
Shipped
 To Africa

Junk thrown
 In rivers
Drinking waters
Sprayed on trees
Thrown In seas
Killing fish
Threatening
The planet
And everything in it

We must overcome
Junk In the mind
 Heart
Body and soul
Junk in homes
In attics
Basements
Under beds
In sheds
And kitchen cupboards

Junk pile high
Miles wide
In streets and alleys
Some places
On this lovely planet
Junk born
From inspiration
In condemnation
Or appreciation
In art exhibitions

Junk that leaves
No room
In life for better
Opportunities

Junkie's mother
Cries, no help
Loses self-control

We must overcome
Oppression
Abduction of children
Teen runaways
Cocaine babies
Border babies
Cloned babies
Baby pornography
Indentured servitude
 In Haiti

We must overcome
Child labor
World hunger
Children born
Deformed
 By war chemicals
 in Fallujah

Female Disempowerment

We must overcome
Sex slaves
Rape
Human trafficking
Women and children
 Living on $2 a day
 Globally, struggling
Through endless
Wars and calamities
Brought on them by
Corporate colonialism

We must overcome
Patriarchal superiority
Man's ego
Threatened
Honor killings
Goes unpunished
Victims' graves
Left unmarked
No one visits
No justice

We must overcome
Female disempowerment
By disfigurement
This calamitous disgrace
Of throwing acid
 In a woman's face
If she refuses a man
In marriage

Asserting her
 Independence
Is a crime
Dishonoring family
Is a grave tragedy

A woman suffers
Forever
If she refuses a marriage
Her parents
Arranged for her
To a man
Before she even
 Sees his face

We must overcome
Female disempowerment
By ancient traditions
Women's rights
And freedoms
Hijacked by men
No legal right for women
To defend themselves
Sexual abuse
Deprivation of education
Woman's power seized
By violence, even murder
A girl's childhood is robbed
By early marriage
Her future is uncertain
Her children suffer
From the evils
Of some archaic
Traditions
Still operating
In many modern
Nations

We must overcome
Female disempowerment
By ancient traditions
In Africa
Smart beautiful women
Are stuck in dilemma
Of marriage trade
 And poverty
A father's cows
Worth more than a girl
Her dowry is desired
To pay the bride price
Of her brother

 We must overcome
This ancient tradition
Of oppressing woman
In the 21st century

We must overcome
Patriarchal superiority
In Albania
A medieval tradition
Still in operation
A girl is trained
To be a man
If there is no male
To lead the family's clan

She dresses like a man
Do the work of a man
And leads the household
As if she is a man
"When I embarked
On this journey
It became my world
There was no
Turning back"
She sacrificed
Her femininity
For the sake
Of patriarchal
Superiority

We must overcome
Male superiority
 Women! women!!
Everywhere
Do not settle
For subjugation
 Anywhere

Amazing women!
Strong women!
Liberated women!
Fearless women!
Take your liberation
Create super nations
Say no to exploitation
Of any type
Say no to
Male superiority
Settle for nothing
Less than equal rights
And opportunity

Settle for nothing less than
Respect honor and dignity
Equality and liberty
There is no time
Like the right time
To make a move
 For change the view
Of womankind
Things cannot continue
The same
 Only women can save
This patriarchal world
 Gone insane

Amazing Women*!*
In countries
Where oil wells flow
 And diamonds glow
Do what you need to do
Stop Corporations
From stealing
 Your wealth
And walking free
Leaving you with
Toxic pollution
poverty
And generations
 Of children robed
Of their heredity
 Liberty
limbs
 families
 homes
 lives
 lands
 visions
Humanity

Do you forget?
Don't you remember?
That inhuman behavior
Happened before
Many times, before
Get naked and protest!
Do what works best
Settle for nothing less
But the best

Women! Women!!
Everywhere!
Do not settle
for subjugation
Anywhere

Gunmen loose in Cities

We must overcome
Gunmen
 Loose in cities
Mass murders
 In schools, churches
And bars
Racist attacks
 On holy places
Gang wars
 In crack city
Crack city graffiti

Mob crimes
 Mob terror
Contract murders
Police brutality
In the inner cities
Police chasing
A car jacking
Sniper on the loose
A challenge
For Chief Moose

We must Overcome
Contradictions

Save two elephants
In Kenya
One stranded whale
In Alaska
Kill innocent buffaloes
In Montana
Choose animals to eat
Those to save
From extinction

Ignore genocide in Rwanda
 Send troops to Romania
Israel bombs Palestine
With democracy
 Freedom, dignity
And honor
Gifts to Palestine
 From America
With friendly fire
Britain and France celebrate
Bombing democracy
 Into Libya

We must overcome
Cats and dogs
Sleeping on satin sheets
On antique beds
In their own rooms
Empty houses boarded up
Homeless people
Homeless mothers
Babies, in shelters
On the streets
Parents looking at children
With nothing to feed them

220 million spent
On one football player
I percent of the
Population gets richer
8 men have more money
Than 3.6 billion people
Millions face austerity
Or dying of hunger
Food good for a feast
Are thrown in dumpsters
Contradiction

Male god
Replaced female god
To keep women down
A whole black man
Equals 3/5 white man
In American
Constitution
Bacha boys
Dress like women
In scanty sexy costume
To dance for men
While women cover
Themselves
Even their ears
Contradiction

We must overcome
 Deals
Russian hacking
Not convincing
Peace deal signed
On Syrian war
Rebels deliberating
On a cease fire
Weapons deal signed
With Saudi Arabia
And America

Send weapons
Around the world
 Peace deals, arms deal
Going on
At the same time

Peace deals
With FAC in Columbia
7000 gorillas
Laid down their arms
For a chance at a comeback
As a civilian
contradiction

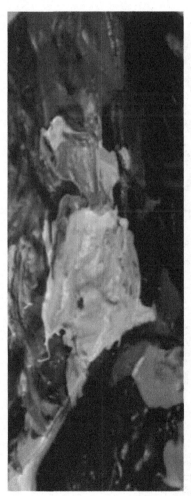

Starve the People

Punish the rebel
Use the rebels
To fight the leaders
Back the bad guys
Send them weapons
Sign million dollars
Weapons deal
With Saudis
One must be blind
Not to see
Such deals
Are not for peace

Wall Street gets bailed out
Bond holders
Are defended
Homeowners thrown
Out of their homes
In the cold
Contradiction

We must overcome

Arms dealers
In charge of peace
Security Council
Unable to act
Men on human
Rights council
Their wives at home
 In bondage
 And oppression

Men deciding
Women's issues
Even those of
 Menstruation
¼ of a million
Mostly black men
Jailed
On Bill Clinton's
Watch
Some
For a few kilos
 Of pot
Contradiction

We must overcome
Smearing
 To conquer
Citizens poisoned
 In Bhopal India
Environmentalist
 Killed
People engaged
 In polluting activities
Hurt Mother earth
With no moral
Or economic
 Responsibility
Condemnation
But no effective
 Negotiation
For a solution
Contradiction

Do Not

Do not establish
 Safe zones
Safe countries
No one will be afraid
 To stay at home

Do not fix
 Bridges
Your thinking
Pot- holes
The system
Do not
Radicalize
 By internet
Listening to others
 Plot hatred
And death

If the government
Does not work
The people say
 They are stealing
The money

Living in the Jungle

We must overcome
Living in the jungle
Fighting imperialism
If a man knows
He will be killed
He may fight back
 Harder still

If a man
 Is willing to die
Do not bomb
 His mother
He may fight back
 Harder
An eye for an eye
A tooth for a tooth
Do not throw stones
If you have
Glass windows

Drums and Rumors of Wars

Got hotter
By the hour
Russia wanted to talk
America wanted to walk
Kim Jung Un
 Wanted to test missiles
 To save North Kore
 From America
Emanuel Macron
Wanted to make
 The planet great
Donald trump
 Wanted to make
 America great again

The big bad west
With the biggest
 War ships and under-
water submarines
Grandstands in the Korean
 Peninsulas and black sea
Alliance of the strong
Against the weak
The strong willing
 To do anything
For total domination
Of all nations

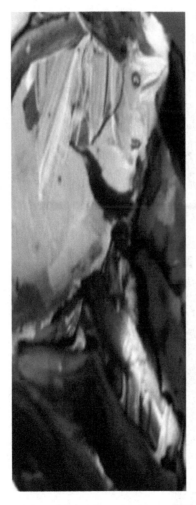

Friends Like You
Make Friends Like us
Look Bad

Qatar
 Unafraid
 Of blockade
No longer trusted
Her longtime friends
They ganged up
And accused her
Of supporting terror
They cut off her air, sea,
 land and water ports
Saudi cut off
 Her only land
 Routes for 40 %
Of her food
Terrorism!
Terrorism!
Her friends shouted
It's terrorist like you
Make terrorist like us
 Look bad

Corruption

We must overcome
World racketeering
Cyber hacking
Offshore banking
Crazy woman laughing
At a leader's beheading
Pharmaceuticals
Having the medicine
For the perfect psycho

Offshore swindlers
Getting mining deals
In Katanga Zaire
1.7 million Zairians died
No roads no access
To clean water
Chemical waste
Are emptied in their rivers

Greed and death in Congo
Highway robbery in Puerto Rico
Worthless bonds
For mom and pop
From Goldman's sacks
In New York

Corrupt Democracy

We must overcome
Democracy in which
Candidates' bomb
Their way in
And out of power
Democracy
 In which candidates
Make changes
 To the constitution
To rule forever

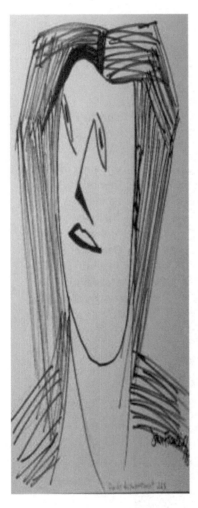

Poverty

Who cares?
 About the poor?
Morality or soul
Why are the poor
Poor?
Who cares?
 About the poor?
Who are the rich?
Do rich know
 What poor is?
If they've never
Been without a bite
When they open
Their fridge
All is well inside
Who cares?
 About the poor?
Reverend
 William Barber
I am sure

Listen up!
Listen up!
Listen--------- up!
It is a Plot
Things are Like That

Wherever There is Light

Study
 Where there is light
Light is a factor
Water is a factor
Roads are a factor
Health is a factor
When Government
Running things
Is a disaster

 Study with friends
At petrol stations
Or at airports
 Wherever there
 Is electric light
When Government
Running things
Is a disaster

Fear of Food

We must overcome
Fear of food
Not sure
 If it is from a can
Or natural
Not sure which ones
 Have pesticides
Genetically modified
Or DNA altered

Not sure
 If it is salmon
  From the ocean
Or a fish
 From a farm

We must overcome
Weed killer in foods
And on the lawns
Shining is the apple
Of the eye
No longer smells
Sweet as a pie

269

Artificial Intelligence

We must
Overcome
Artificial
Intelligence
We do not know
How robot
Will interfere
We will not know
The difference
 Between
Bionic
Or real human
Forget about
The new thing
Called texting
Plant a chip
In your brain
And do
 Technological
Telepathy
 Instead

Television Brainwashing

We must overcome
Television
Brainwashing
Television crime
They tell you
What to think
What to say
What to believe
Come what may
How to wear
 Your hair
What to wear
 Each day

They tell you
Close your eyes
 And pray
They tell you truth
They tell you lies
Not to give
You do not know
 Who he is?

Hatred and Ignorance
We must overcome
Hatred
 Ignorance
Racial exterminating
Racism
Dehumanizing
Anti-Semitism
Right wing
Extremism
Domestic terrorism
Racial profiling
Exceptionalism

Disliking, destroying
Who gave the right?
To destroy Palmira
To erode female
Influence forever
Middle East on fire
Nothing but ecological
Disaster
What are you in the fight for?
Oil, minerals ego, or blood?

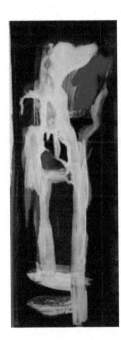

Monkey Business

We must overcome
False history
False news
Mental slavery
Mass psychology
Media propaganda
Covering
 Big blunders
Rat race
 Capitalism
Corporate
 Takeovers
By rich
 Aggressors
Subprime
 Highway robbers
Too big to fail
Too big for jail
White collar
Criminals
Stealing
 From the poor
White collar criminals
Don't go to jail

Prison Slaves

We must overcome

Prison populations for
Modern slave
Institutions
To stop black male
Liberation
Human
Experimentation
Without
Notification

We must overcome
Scandals in the Catholic
Church
In the white house
War against
Whistle blowers
Whistle blowers
Killed or jailed
Truth cannot be unveiled
Free speech
And transparency
Is a 21st century
Luxury

We Must Overcome Weapons

Weapons
Proliferation
No moral
 Obligation
Weapons
 Of mass
Destruction
Scud missiles
Nerve gas
Depleted
 Uranium
Acid rain
Barrel bombs
Trident two
Nuclear weapons
Designed
To obliterate
Entire nations

Bombs Rained on Iraq

Demonstrations
 In New York
Precision bombs
Smart bombs
Heavy artillery
B3 bombers
Tomahawk missiles

588 bombs dropped
 On cities
 Waters, roads and bridges
Laser guided, precise
Outmatched
 Overmatched
With domination
And supremacy

Thousands died
Before they could
 Ask why?
What an operation
Of destruction
Of a nation

Explosions
Rocked Bagdad
Like something
Out of Star Wars
Two weeks
Of pounding
Left mother earth
Lamenting

Bagdad burned
Children cried
Plumes of smoke
Shot up
Suffocated babies
Clutching
Their mothers

Innocent people
Blasted into pieces
Fathers
In the frontline
Widows
Orphans
Left behind
In the rubble

Bomb Raids

Combat attack
Sirens sounds
Civilians
 Hit the ground
Cruise missiles
Light up the sky
Nowhere to hide
Its liberation
 Of a nation

Bombs
 In the right hand
Food in the left
Justice from the west
Democracy, freedom
Dignity, and honor
Arrived in Bagdad
From Britain
And America
With friendly fire

From Basra
 To Nasiriyah
Kirkuk to Mosul
Kuwait to Bagdad

Raqqa to Aleppo
Mosul to Yemen
Wisp of breaths
Smelt like death
Bomb! Bomb! Bomb!
Says Johnny, bomb!
 As much as you can
Kill with any weapon
Except
 Chemical weapons
Its political evolution
American
 e x c e p t I o −
 a l I s m
Nationalism
Self-exaltation
Global
Totalitarianism
Super nation
Are US
 A young bully?
Spreading western
 Democracy

No Condition Worked

16 years invasion

Cost one hundred
 Billion
To create
A new Afghanistan
Bomb! Bomb!
Says Jonny

Donald Trump
Dropped
mother bomb
 On Afghanistan
A large bomb
Cost 314 million
Mother earth
Trembled from
Ferocious pounding
From a destroyer
An imposter
A betayer
Doing evil
 In the name
of *mother*
No condition
Worked

Illegal Occupation
We must
 Overcome
Israel's occupation
 Of Palestine lands
Violence
On temple Mt.
Jews and Muslims
Clash over
The right
To god's house
Two thousand
 Prisoners
 On hunger strike
Held without trial
Infringement on
 Their human rights
Israel punishes
With immunity
Children and adults
 No distinction
In their west bank
Open prison
 Operations

The Evils Men do

We must overcome
 Droning
Ghetto bird spying
Big brother watching
Bio magnetic drones
Drone striking
Drone executions
Unmanned drones
Sophisticated
 Killers
Over Yemen
Syria, Iraq
 And Libya
Somalia
 Pakistan
And Afghanistan
How do
 The women feel?
How many men
Are left to heal

Secret Prisons

We must
Overcome
Secret prisons
One sided
Hague court
Justice
Oligarchy
NASR
Abu grebe
Skid row
Guantanamo

Water boarding
Choke holding
Torturing
Hunger striking
Anal feeding
Isle's beheadings
Boko Haram
Kidnappings
Bombings
Fighting
Terrorism

Collateral Damage

Millions die
Before sunset
And sunrise
A Mosque
Is bombed
Men dug
In the debris
For loved ones
A Woman
Screamed
Cannot take it
Anymore!
God!
Where are you?
Tell me what to do!

Opposition
And moderate
Rebels armed
Troops
On the ground
Who rules?
Depends on
Which rebel
They choose

Do the Math

Two wrongs
Do not make right
Obama dropped
3 bombs an hour
24 hours a day
Equals what?
Death
 And destruction

72 bombs a day
 Equals what?
Children!
The answer is?
30,000 bombs
 In 2016
Where do
The children play
Where do
 The children go.
Why are
 The children not here?
They have gone
To graveyards
 Everywhere

A Great Pretender

Two faced politicians
Lies a lot
Peace needs a plan
Not weapons
Millions in the street
Demonstrating

150 died in a flood
A few hundred buried
When the mountain
Tumbled down
In a Chinese village
Hundreds died
When the hill
Came down
In Sierra Leon

Two men killed
By white supremist
Defending a Muslim
Woman
Do not talk of wars
Or illegal wars
America is a great
Pretender

Stand up for Standing Rock

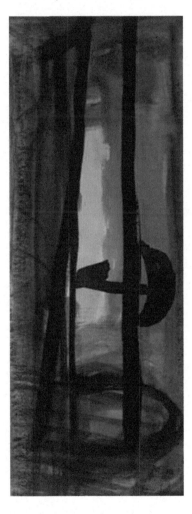

Stand up
 For the rights
Of standing rock
Dakota access
 Pipeline
Multi-million
 Dollar
Project
 Through sacred
 Land
Threatens water
For 18 million
Indigenous
Americans

Pepper spray
 Attack dogs
Set on water
Protectors
Little hope
For future
Generations
Of standing rock
Nation

Globalism

We must
Overcome
Global warming
World hunger
Aids, cancer
Ebola, malaria
Chicken Bunya
Zika, Covid 19
Domestic
Political
Dysfunction
Inequality
Of opportunity
Patriarchal
Superiority
 Bigotry
Cocaine
 In Columbia
Starvation
 In Ethiopia
Slavery
 In Sudan
Hegemony
 Oligarchy
Anarchy

Fences and Walls

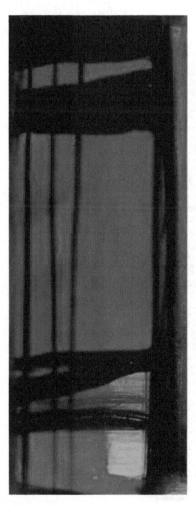

We must overcome
Wars on refugee
 And migrants
One hundred
Surveillance cameras
Monitor the ports
Concrete
And metal fences
Barbed wire
Green zone
High tech fence
Virtual surveillance
Drone raiders
Tall walls
With sharp spikes
Security fence act
Two hundred billion
Not too much
For security
 And liberty
Border security
 Is big business
Imagine
Putting all that money
Into good senses
Jobs and opportunities

Kiss me Quickly!

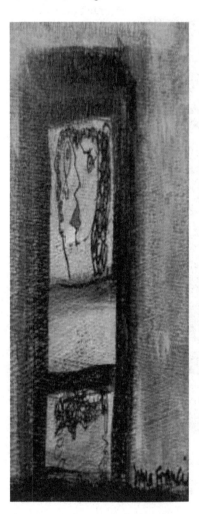

Before the Border Gate Closes

Do you take this man?
 As your husband
Do you take
 This woman?
 As your wife
Kiss quickly
Before the gate
Closes
One year before
 It opens again

Here is something
 For mama
Something for pappy
 For our babies
This! for you
My lovely seniority
Kiss me! Hug me tight
Here he comes
I will dream of you
Every night
I love you baby!

Star Wars

We must overcome
War in El Salvador
War in the east
War in the west
Cold wars
Mistaken wars
 Regional wars
Punitive wars
Wars of conquest
Wars for oil
Proxy wars
100 year's wars
13 years wars costing
Trillions of dollars
Destabilize
 Not recognize
Overthrow
And behead leaders
Wreck nations
Create failed states
And sectarianisms
Turn cities into rubble
And citizens into rebel

Operation Fears

We must overcome
Operation Just Cause
Cast lead
Shock and awe
Iron Foot
 Desert storm
Anaconda
 Fear
 Sombrero
Top Kill

World trade center
Tumbled down
Protests erupt
 In Istanbul
Bomb explodes
 In Paris café
Fear of knives, guns
Suicide vests
And truck terrorist

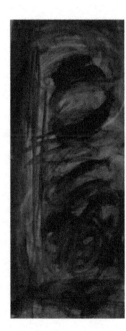

Missiles From the Sky

Phosphorous
And barrel bombs
Rains from the sky
Civilians live
 In constant fear
Yet they say
Do not worry
Live normally
We do not know
who will come?
And when?
Running for your life
When no threat
Is in sight
Do not panic
Soldiers
Are in the square
A few bombs
Are dropped
On a hundred rebels
In Somalia
To neutralize
 The atmosphere

293

Vigilante coast guards
 Ply the seas
Adjust your mood
Watch
 Every small road
 No credible threats
But be on the alert
Careful how you talk
Watch
Where you walk
Look around you
Run and hide
Report
 What you see

Crowd's panic
All events canceled
Schools Locked down
A town stands still
Mother said
Watch your back

Earth's Exploitation

We must overcome
Earth's exploitation
Three thousand
Barrels of crude
Burned
In the Mexican gulf
Frocking
Wherever they can

Carbon overheating
Radioactive waste
Seeping
In ground water
Low grade fly ash
8000 died
Toxic chemicals
Poison leaking
In drinking water
Factories
Still operating
In Bhopal India

People Against Mother Earth

We must overcome
People engaged in
 Polluting activities
Hurt mother earth
With no moral or
 Economic
 Responsibility
Environmentalist
 Are killed
Fighting against
Global exploitation
The world
 Is like a chess game
Evil is winning

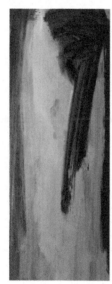

Offshore Exploitation

We must overcome
Exploitations
By multinational
Corporations
Cheap labor
Blood diamonds
Black gold
Chemical wastes
Create toxic city
In Accra, Nigeria
And Cameroon

Send bombs
And other
 Weapons
Offshore
Grow food
Off-shore
Get mineral
Resources
Offshore

Gold, silver
Diamonds
Iron ore
Manganese
Aluminum
 Lead
Bauxite
 copper
Petroleum
 Uranium
 Coal and tin
 Comes from
 Offshore
All the metals
In your cell phone
 Comes from
 Offshore
Question more
Ask where is
Off- shore
Is it no man's land?
Where one can
Grab all one can
Or
Is it Africa?

Consumerisms

We must overcome
Consumerisms
Eat all you can
From the buffet
 Stand
Try a deep dish
Whenever
 You can
Or ger a six-piece Popeye
With some fries
Wash it down
With a 16 oz
Lose the weight
 In a week
Try the twenty
One day program
Or call Jenny
Its capitalism
Its democracy
Its freedom
Eat and be merry

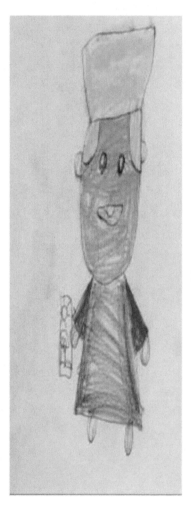

Millionaire Leader

Millionaire leader
Capable looser
Reality tv star
Sports topes, yellow
Is his favorite color
He hates the media
Strongly claiming
fake news
Is all they conspire

He tweets in all caps
 At the mid night hour
And incites insurrection
On the US Capital
To seize power

He gave power
 To the people
In words and lies
And dollars
 To billionaires
In contracts
 And small taxes

300

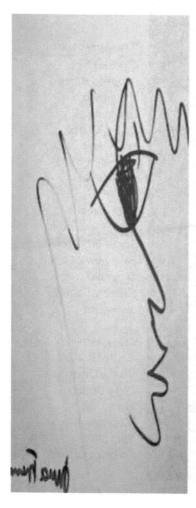

He sets up baby jail
And zero tolerance
To stem illegal immigration
At the US Mexican border
He ate sweet
Chocolate-cake
With Xi Jinping
At the same time
He missile strike
Poor Syria

He promised to drain
The government swamps
Drained it he did
And filled it back
Only with those
Willing to do his bidding

He lost an election
Rebuked his defeat
And desperately tried
Cheating
To retain the seat

301

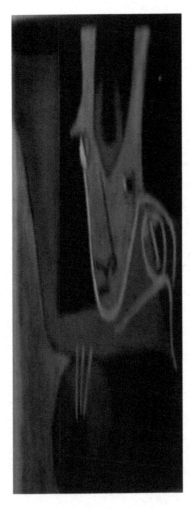

Trumpmockisms
Fire and fury
Crooked Hilary
Little Marco
Lyin ted
Crying Chuck
Low energy Jeb
Crazy Jim
Psycho Joe

Rocket man
Sloppy Brannon
Tricky dick female
Fake news
Slime ball
Slippery Comey
Sleepy joe

Crazy Bernie
Goofy Elizabeth
Wacky Omarosa
Dicky Durbin
Flakey jeff
Moonbeam Brown
Wild Bill
Cheating Obama

PART Ten: Voices of the People

Let your voice be heard
Millions of ways
To reach the world
Tell the people
What's going on

Let Your Voice be Heard

Let your voice
 Be heard
Millions of ways
To reach the world
Tell people
What's going on
Don't be afraid
Express your First
Amendment
 Rights

The world is
Changing fast
Communication
Has reached
A technological
 Revolution

Use websites
Emails
 Snapchats
Face Book
WhatsApp
Twitter
Instagram

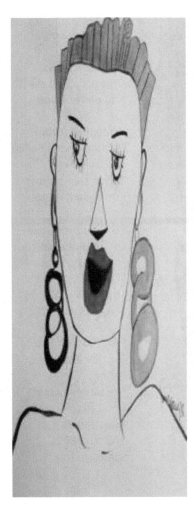

QQ
Ozone
Flicker
Skype
Linked
Or Pinterest

Write a poem
 Sing a song
Etch a tattoo
 On your arm
Write a note
For Hopes Tree
Tell it in a video
 In your own
 Documentary

Drop leaflets
Write articles
Hang banners
Nail a poster
On the border
Wall near Tijuana
In San Diego

Hang it on a big
 Building
On a metro bus
On delivery trucks
And on rooftops

Write it in graffiti
On abandoned buildings
And in alleys
Turn a shanty town
Into a giant mural

Post your message
On the sidewalk
At the stop light
When people wait
They look down
They will read it

Post it on billboards
Outside a window
Facing
The busiest street
Don't forget radio
Newspapers
And television
Some are free

Tell it any way you can
Make sure people get it
Call public meetings
 Use a megaphone
Shout it though
 A bullhorn
In the world's
Busiest squares

In Tiananmen
Red Square
St Peters square
Castle square
Trafalgar square
 Place Des Vosges
Madison square
 Garden
In mid- town
 Manhattan

Hide Park in London
Tahrir square, Cairo
 Dundas In Toronto
Independence
 In Ghana West Africa

Asmara in Eritrea
Addis Ababa Ethiopia
Kampala Uganda
Dodoma
In Tanzania
Mogadishu
In Somalia
Ouagadougou
In Burkina Faso

Go to downtown
Detroit
Don't miss
Broadway in
New York City
Go to every plaza
Wherever they are

San Marco
Di Spagna
Del Campo
De Espana
Calanques
De Piana

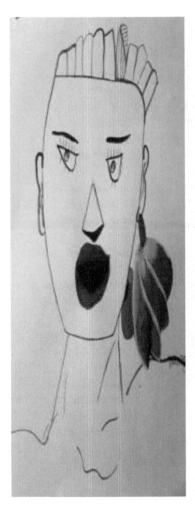

Asco Piazza
In Zimbabwe
At Nanjing Road
In Shanghai
Grand Parade
In Cape Town
In Port of Spain
Trinidad and Tobago
St Georges Grenada
Carriacou
And Petite Martinique
Bridge Town Barbados
Freetown Sierra Leon
Georgetown Guyana
Lagos
And Port Harcourt
Nigeria
Dakar Senegal

Tell the people
One by one
Or all at once
A million
Or more ways
To reach them all

Take your issue
 To the judges
On the people's
Court
Baby daddies
Are found
On Morrie Povich
DNA drama

Go to Jerry Springer
 If it's to claim
Your lover
Oy your husband
From a husband snatcher
Tell them If the deal
 You get Is unfair

Message to the Queen

First
Take a message to
The queen of England
Have a woman to woman
 Talk with the woman
 She is unaware
 The sun has set

Let her know
It is time for her
To give the castle
To the people
It is time
To stop being *the queen*

It is time for her
To start a royal
Woman's revolution
For a just global civilization
Where all women are free
And treated equal
With dignity

Hopeless
Hungry
Homeless Britons
lined the streets
To watch her
Wearing a hat
That cost
A million pounds
In her grandson's
Wedding
That cost
45 million dollars

Tell her it's shameful
To keep wearing
That jeweled
Crown of shame
It is time to
Decolonize her mind
And the people
And end her
Undemocratic privileges

It is time to decolonize
The history books
Glorify heroes
Of human rights
 Build truth museums
To differentiate
Criminals from heroes

Tell her
In a liquor store
 One day
A woman
 From Sierra Leonian
Was heard saying
Queen Elizabeth
 wears
 Sierra Leon's jewels
 On her head

Tell the lady
It's time for a reckoning
With people
Still suffering
From colonialism

She needs to free
 Herself
From an immoral
 Emblem

Crown or no crown
People know she is a
Queen colonizer
Wearing a crown
Of jewels
That doesn't belong
 To England or her
While the people
 Suffer from shelter
And hunger

Let her know
It is not too late
For a new vision
For her nation
Not too late to face
The inconvenient
 Truth, of the evils
Of colonial empires
Please! tell the lady!

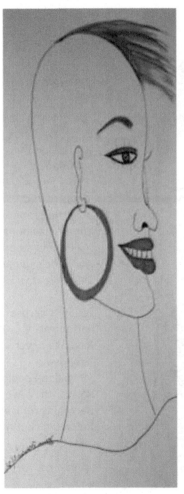

Our Stories

Let your voice
 Be heard
Say what's on
 Your mind
Tell it
 Like it is
Don't
 Change
The facts
Don't be
 Ashamed
Don't mind
You may
Get blamed

Tell the people
How you wished
You never lived
When strangers
with all kinds
Of weapons
Turned your
Country into
A battle-ground
Tribes, coalitions
Allies', neighbors
And rebels fought
To the death

Leader's corpse
left to rot
Revenge never
Stopped
65 million People
Ran for their lives
Becoming refugees
In foreign countries

316

Tell the People
like You Told Me

Nightmares
Haunt my life
Of things
I never dreamed
I'd lived to see

Something died
 Inside me
To see
My beloved city
In ruins
And turmoil

I spent a night
 In a forest
 With smugglers
 Strangers claiming
To know a way
To a safer place

I just
Want
The
Bombs
 To stop falling
I only want
Peace

I did not start
The war
I just need
A little chance
 To carry
 On my life

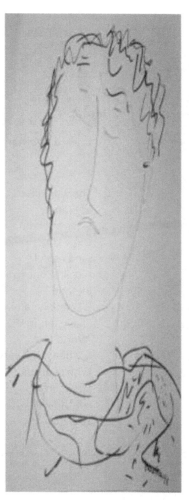

I am a mother

The war took
My children
My family
My home
My community
My country

My world
Has turned
Upside down
Martyrdom
 Is my only
 Consolation

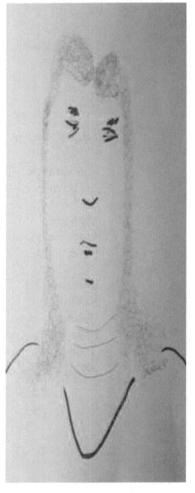

319

I am a Woman

The war killed
My family
I was pulled
Out of my Home
And raped
A child Conceived
By rape
Is the only family
I have left in the
World
My heart is weary
With sadness
Struggling
For the will
To persevere

Woman In War Zone

I Live
 In a war zone
Red flames
Rain down
 On us
Explosives
Planted
On the roads
Killed my sons

Long days
And nights
No sleep
No food
My children
 Are tired
 And afraid

I envy the dead
I see no hope
I see no light
At the end
Of a dreary dark tunnel

Woman in War Zone

I am caught
In a war
Fear
Hopelessness
Anxiety
And depression
Saturate my being

If I go outside
I might die
If I stay inside
I might die

I see no way
Out of mayhem
No future
For my children
I feel dead
 Already

Woman in Bondage

I am a
Housewife
A woman
In bondage
By traditions

Caught
In a mix
Of wealth
Slavery
And luxury

No one
To turn to
No human
Rights
I ran away
To save my life

Baby's Mama

I am a teenager
I was rejected
By my family
They claimed
I dishonored
Them
With an unwed
Pregnancy

My family
Many families
In my country
live in superficial
Reality
In which a price
Is put
On a girl's virginity

Baby's Mama

I am sixteen
I was unable to protect
My priceless virginity

I was raped by my father
Raped a second time
By some boys
Stained, pregnant
And considered unfit
My mother rejected me
She drove me from home
Left me hopeless
Powerless

I have no idea
What my future
Will be
What will become
Of my baby and me

Baby' Mama

My parents
 Found
I was pregnant
And drove me
 From home
An enlightened
Mama
 In a rejected
Girl' center
Rescued me
From imposed
Homelessness
And more
Impending
Disaster
She gave me
 Hope
And a light
Towards
 My future

Child Bride
Because I am a girl
I was considered
A liability
My family
Married me
Before I turned
Ten
To an old man
With several
Children

Centuries old
Traditions
Shaped
My destiny
Education
Or no education
Girls like me
Must change
This unfortunate
legacy

Cursed Girl

I am
 Madagascan
I am considered
An abomination
A cursed child
Because I am
A twin

I was abandoned
 At birth
Made a living sacrifice
Forced into sexual
Servitude in a shrine
To appease Gods
And ancestors
For family crimes

Girl Victim

I am Nigerian
Boko Haram
Kidnapped me
And one hundred
More girls
The rebels
Killed
My friend
They left me for dead
I survived
To tell the world
To stop this crime

Girl Victim

I am a girl
A victim
Of ancient
Traditions

My family
Threatened
To set me
On fire
If I refused
To marry
The man
They chose
For me

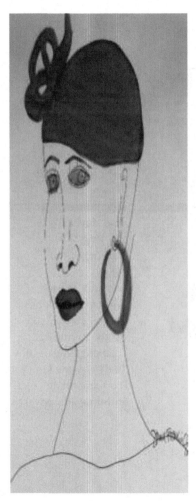

I am Haitian

My family died
In a mega-earthquake
Help came to Haiti
from far away
I was forced to give
The helper's sex
For money
Before
They helped me

I am Guatemalan

I was smuggled
By traffickers
To America
I made a move
To help my family
Only to end up
In bondage
And slavery
Working
Against my will

I did not foresee
What life might be
When I embarked
On the journey
To change my destiny
To deliver my family
From unending
Suffering and poverty

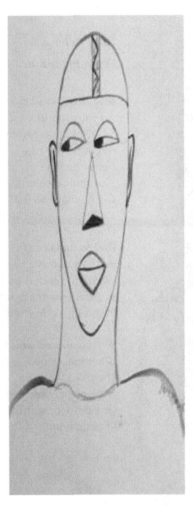

I am a Broken Man

A Rwandan
Rebels gave me
Ten seconds to choose
Bullets or machete
For them to kill
My wife

I am a broken man
Unable to understand
What nature conspired
That day travesties
Descended
On my country

Where can a man
In my situation
Find strength
To live on

What do I tell?
My children
To console them
I am a broken man

I am Rohingya
From Myanmar

My village was burnt
To the ground
5,000 pregnant women
Went on the run
Genocide
Or ethnic cleansing
Call it what you like

One million of us
Fled to Ban la dash
But ban La Dash
Wants to send us back
We are denied a place
In this big wide world

What a wicked world
What makes people do
The things they do
Is it lack of conscience?
Or a more powerful
Phenomenon

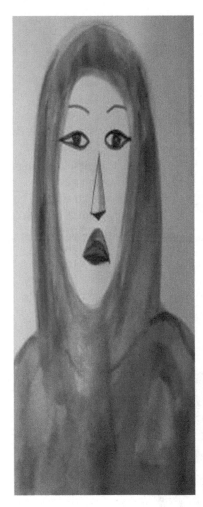

I am Rohingya
From Myanmar

I am sixteen
I was raped
By soldiers
They killed
 My parents
 In front of me
Aung San Suu Kyi
Nobel peace prize
 Winner
 Trapped
 Under the spell
Of the mighty
Military
Was unable
 To protect
 Women
And girls
Like me

I am a Refugee Boy

Caught in a booming
Organ trade
Organ trafficking
Human trafficking
Body parts sold
For survival
I was forced
To sell my Kidney
To feed my family

Sweet, sweet

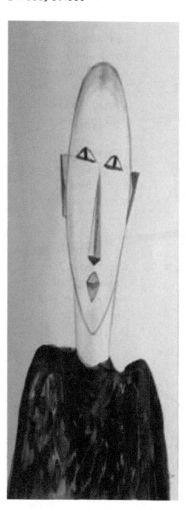

Chocolate

I am a small boy
I live with my family
In utter poverty
I have never eaten
A bar of chocolate
I haven't
A pair of shoes
I don't go to school

Boys like me
One million of us
From Ghana
And Ivory Coast
Some of us
Trafficked
Work illegally
No pay
From dawn to dust
On cocoa farms
I have never eaten
A bar of chocolate

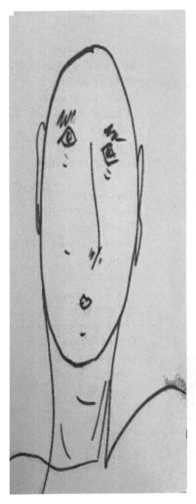

I am Palestinians

I am a Palestinian
Living under
 Criminal occupation
I am stuck
Behind a wall
 140 square miles long

I live in an open-air prison
Blocked by air, sea, land
Buffer zone
 And electric fence

Despair, desperation
Oppression
Check-point humiliation
Unending misery
That killed my family
And keeps me down
Is all I know

Bloodshed in Gaza

Occupiers and protesters
Marched
Against each other
Rocks and stones
Against bombs, shrapnel
Live bullets, tear gas
And water cannon

Brimstone and fire
 Stampede and terror
 David against goliath
Resistance against repression

Dozens killed
Thousands maimed
Young men got shot
In the back
Running from the fire
Massacre with impunity
No hope, no opportunity
No future in Gaza

I am American

I am America

I was born
Amid violence
I lived in squalid
Below the poverty
Line
With few legal rights

Searching
For a better life
Felt like a crime
Redlining black
Homeownership
Kept me in distress

I was forced to live
In the ghetto
I tried to move
To a so called
Rich part of town
To live there meant
I had to enter
Through the poor door

340

Innocent men
Get shot down
 In the streets

Where I live
And black men
 Are preferred
By shooters who feel
They have guaranteed
Immunity

I became a victim
 Of police brutality
And unconscious
 Bias
Sleeping in my car
With my black skin color

Watch your back
Mama said
Down that road
 Evil is waiting
For an opportunity
Don't let it be you

I am America

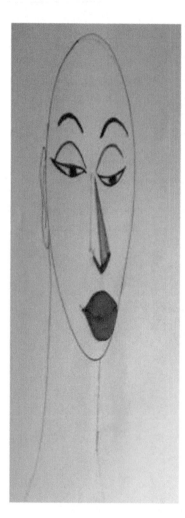

I am an America
I live in Baltimore
Always afraid
 To go out my door

Always afraid
If I have to call the police
I might be framed
With a BB
Or some drugs

No justice
On my street
Police cannot be trusted
Innocent or guilty
Prison waits for me
I am a black man
Living in fear
Hope has escaped me

342

I am American

I am an America

I never thought
I would be homeless
Searching
For a place to rest

My mama
Was a druggie
I was picked on
I was bullied
I sank deep in deeper

I was unable to think
Yet I had to figure out
What to do
To fix my destiny
I felt like a dead
Person walking

I am America
I am an America

I feel like a cow
I get my income
Donating blood

I truly search
For a way out of
Wretchedness

On the streets
People look at me
Some know my calamity
Prejudiced ones
Would rather not see me

I have never
Committed a crime
I am an innocent man
Seeking my destiny
In a system
Built against me

Inside me is a light
It sustains my will
And mountain of faith
To carry on

I am America

I am an America
I live in a beautiful city
 Named New Orleans
I live in substandard
Conditions
Designed for poor
 Black people
Like me

Twelve family members
Got killed
Poo,r black, who cares?
Shoot to kill a black man
A priest ran out of space
Recording victim's names
On his church
God must be asleep

I am American
I am an America
Brothers are dead
 Or locked up
Coming home from prison
They meet 47,000 statutory
 Barriers
That Keep them down

I live in terror, of sirens
 And rolling lights
Intimidating
My neighborhood
All the time

When I see a black man
Frisked by the police
I immediately
Imagine the worst
If he Is pined to the ground
Not even my prayers
Would help
He may never
Get up again

Innocent or guilty
His destiny
Could easily be
Death or prison
One America
Two systems
Of justice
One exclusively
 For men of color

If one is black
And moreover
Poor
Justice gets harder
 By the hour
Some say
We have come
 A long way
But the bars
 Move higher
Each day
Every step
Of the way

347

I am American

My name is
Ahmadu Arbury
I am dead
Because
Of a hate crime
Jogging
 In the morning
With my black
 Skin color

Three white men
 Devoid of conscience
 Lacking humanity
Imbued with hatred
And ignorance
Ambushed and killed me

They're in jail
I am dead
What was their purpose?
What devil made them do it

I am American

My name is
Trayvon Martin

The police shot me dead
Walking with my hoodie
In my black skin color
I was only 17

I am American

My name is Jacob Blake
From Kenosha Wisconsin
I am a victim
 Of unconscious bias
And police brutality
The police shot 7 bullets
 Into my back
In front of my children

Imagine
After they paralyzed me
The hospital shackled me
To the bed
Did they think
I would get up and run
 What's behind this logic?

Nothing but deliberate
Indifference
Racism without
An ounce of feeling

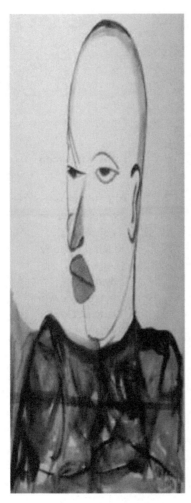

I am American

**My name is
George Perry Floyd**

I am dead
A white policeman
 Knelt on my neck
 For eight minutes
And snuffed
My life out of me
Because
Of my skin color
He did not mind
The world looked on

What's behind this action?
Nothing but deliberate
Indifference
Racism without
An ounce of feeling

I am American

My name is
Gianna Floyd
A policeman
Killed my daddy

"My daddy
Changed the world"
Friend of Floyd's
"I've seen
A grown man cried
Before he died
"Mama!
They're killing me
I can't breathe"
He cried

I am American

I am an America
From Louisville
 Kentucky
My name is
Breonna Taylor
I am dead
A policeman
Sprayed
Eight bullets
Through my door
And into my body
He took my dreams
He snatched
 My destiny
I was only 26
I was a victim
Of deliberate
 Indifference
And police brutality

I am American

I am the soul
 Of black folks
Lifting voices
Singing
For justice
Freedom
And equality
Since the
Beginning
Of Modern
Civilization

I am the soul
 Of black folks
Lifting voices
Singing
For truth
Deprogramming
And Decolonialization

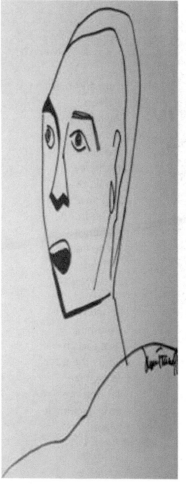

I am American

I am an America
Racist thinkers
 See me as
Who knows what?
Before they know me
Because of the coat
 I wear
Because I have black skin
And braids in my hair
Because I wear a hoody

 Because of how
 I sound black
Without knowing
The goodness in my heart
They are not bred to see
Anything good about me

355

I am an America

I am an American
Racism
 Will not give me
A chance
 To belong
A chance
 To work
A chance
To be free
A chance
To be heard

I do not want
Anyone
To give me
 Anything
 But racism
Shuts the door
In my face
To stop me
From getting it
Myself

I am American

I am a black woman
Racist's thinkers
 see me
 Differently
It does not
Phase me
At all
Will not
 Determine
The way
I should be

I am African
Not happy?
Sorry!
Some may feel
 Like hurting me
They see me
 As a political
 liability
An awareness
Of their forefathers
Crimes
 And liabilities

I am American

I was born
In the ghetto
Guns, poverty
Substandard
Everything
Is all I knew

I had a nine to five
Minimum wage
Could not pay
My rent
When water got
More than flour
And my back
Against the wall
I became
A Sugar Baby
For economic
Security

I am American

Starvation wages
Trailer Park Living
The rich get richer
The poor get poorer
Credit till death
 Do I part
I cannot see it
 Getting better
 I Joined the poor
People's revolution
Hoping to find
 A solution

I am American

I became homeless
And the city's
 Blight
Good Samaritan Elvis
 Summons
Built me a tiny house

I felt some safety
 Some dignity
For a flicker
The city said
I could not keep
 My little security
 Around

They made me
Homeless again
Roaming for a
Safe spot
To lay my head
And dream
For a place
 To home

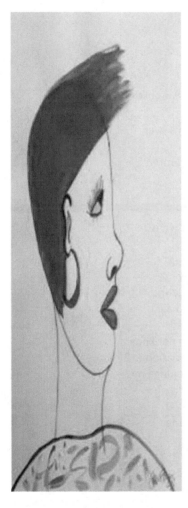

I am American

The sound
The sound
The sound
That rebound
Waiting for Help

Sugar you next!
Well honey!
This is what
You get!
Come back
Next week!

Let me
Connect you
Hold on!
Your ID
Is expired
Sorry!
No opening
Call this number

361

I am American

If you've ever
Been
 Incarcerated
Sorry!
Sorry!
Sorry!
I don't want
Your
 F--------g
Money
You told me
 To find a job
 B -----!
You do not know
 My Situation ... B!
Do not judge me!
Do not
 F--------g
Judge me

I am a Dreamer

I was brought
To America
As a child
I am educated
But have no legal
Documentation
I broke no laws
But I am stuck
In limbo
Living
With endless
Headaches
In the shadows
In fear
And insecurity
Hiding
From deportation
Raids
Waiting
While congress
Debates
The dream act bill

Searching for a Better Life is a Crime

I am Honduran
Mired in pain
Suffering, poverty
And violence
I took a chance
With my children
And headed
For an uncertain
Future In America

I was stopped
At the border
ICE took my children
Shackled my legs
And locked me up
For days, waiting
To face mass trial

Not sure I would see
My children
Or family again
Shattered dreams
Became my reality

I took a chance
A cartel took me
Across a forbidding
River
I climbed a mountain
And walked miles
Across the harsh
Blazing desert
And through
A tangled jungle
With dangerous
Animals

I heard a voice said
Put the body
In a bag, bury it
This is no man's land
I saw many things
I dared to recall
At last, I saw the border wall

Before I could say amen
ICE shackled me
Held me for months
In a detention camp
Charged with a criminal offence

My Name Is Claudia

My name is Claudia
I am Guatemalan
I had a dream
They told me
 I could realize
In America

I took a chance
When I reached
The border
The guards
 Shot me dead

No humanity
Or compassion
At the Rio
Grande
Valley

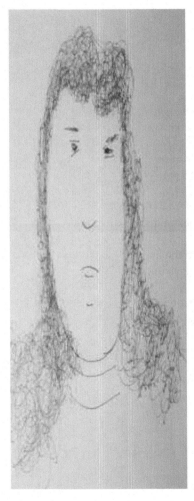

I took a chance
When I saw an opportunity
For my family
To live with dignity
But my dream
Turned to dust
When I overstayed
My documentation

I lived
In the shadows
With nightmares, fear
And insecurity
Endlessly hiding
From Immigration
And deportation

I lived in limbo
Unable to imagine
The direction
My life would go
I had to feed my family
So, I took my chances
Hoping for a miracle
To heal the insanity
That came upon me

I took a chance
I left behind
Poverty
Endlessly misery
Hoping to get
To the land
 Of brave, free
And opportunities

I reached the border
 At the Rio Grande
 Valley
I sat on a bridge
In the burning sun
Three days
Before ICE sent me
Packing
 Back to hell
And the cartel

I saw no future
Earning a salary
 Of misery
Working
 In a mineral mine
For a Yankee dollar

Hope seems far away
Thinking of the dirty air
My children breathe
When they go
Out to play
I would rather die
Trying for a better life

I took a chance with
Zero tolerance
When I arrived at
The Rio Grande valley
Border wall is all
 I could see, before
ICE shackled me
Charged me with a
Criminal offence

I had big dreams
But no opportunity
 In sight
Tired of digging
In the dump
To find something
To sell
I would rather die
 Trying for a better life

I took a chance
Facing death
In the Mexican
Desert
To reach America

My dreams turned
To ashes at the border
I found neither
Compassion nor justice
I was charged
With a criminal offence
And thrown into
ICE detention camp

I am a Refugee

I was forced to choose
Between feeding
 My family
Or fighting
 For workers' rights
To ask for a raise
Risked getting shot at
By my crazy boss

Stuck in a low paid job
With poverty and hardship
Wi-fe and children
Steering me in the face
I would rather die trying
For a better life

I embarked on a journey
Marko Polo
Might have feared
 When finally
I arrived at the border
ICE jailed me

Call me what you like, refugee or migrant

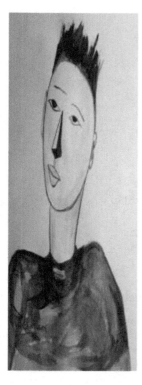

I am a Refugee

In my country
I lived on top of minerals
Some are used
To make cell-pones
Yet, I lived in constant
 Blackout
And endless poverty

Rather than staying
 In the same spot
I would die trying
To find a better life
I took a chance across
The Mediterranean
Hoping to realize my dreams
In a rich foreign land

 I ended up In a Libyan
Slave camp
Where they treat African
refugees like donkeys
They show no solidarity
No mercy

I am a Refugee

My country has
 Gold, diamonds
And other minerals
Yet, I lived
 In constant poverty
With no opportunity
Rather than staying
In the same spot
I would die trying
For a better life

I took a chance across
The Mediterranean
 To a foreign land, in strange
Places, with strangers

Some want me sent back
On the rubber boat
Care not, if I drown or float
Some want me
 Wear a wrist band
To identify me a refugee

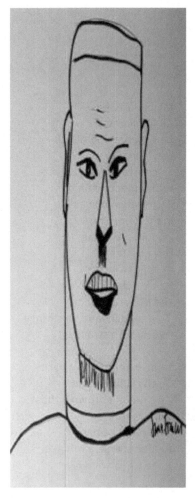

I am an Iraqi Refugee

They spread lies
 And deception
To wage war
On my country
Spent trillions
To kill an old enemy
They claimed, had
 Weapons for mass
 Causality

 Iraq was turned
 Upside down
No weapons were found
Ethnic cleansing
was let loose
Forcing me to run

Smugglers took me
Through the Alps
To get to France
But stole my money
 And abandoned me
In the mountains

374

I am a Refugee

Many people
Despise refugees
Do they think refugees
Are adventurous marauders
Plying dangerous seas
Treacherous mountains
And trekking through
Scorching deserts

Refugees are people
Fleeing death
Dehumanization
Deportation
Burdened with worries
About family
How to get food
And where to sleep safely

Refugees are people
With dreams
Seeking a chance
To be believed
A chance at human rights
A chance for a better life

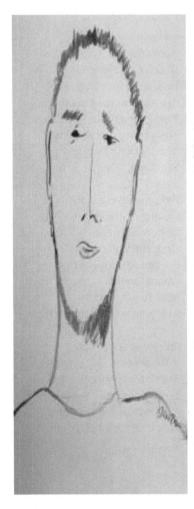

I am a Refugee

I embarked
On a journey
To escape
Pain, misery
And poverty

Fifteen of us
In the same
Predicament
Sleep on one
Tattered blanket
Under a bridge

We share stories
Comfort each other
Talk of death, life
What we left behind
How to stay alive
And of people's
Indifference
To our plight

I am a Refugee

I am a refugee
Living illegally in Italy
In a shack, in a shanty
I left home
Running from poverty
And no opportunity
My vision was to help
My family, from the place
My journey takes me
Sadly, I ended up in slavery
With slavers whose only
Concern was making money

It broke my heart
To see the coldness
In their eyes
I shuddered
At the harsh sound
Of their voices
Ordering people around
I watched them turn off
Humanity
And switched to cruelty
All because of money

I am a Refugee

My whole family
Was buried alive
Under rubble
In Mosul
I am the only one
Left struggling
To stay alive

I took a chance
Crossed
The Mediterranean
And the Black Sea
Hoping to find
Liberty, peace
And security

I ended up
In a detention camp
In a foreign country
Wondering
What did I do?
Where did I go wrong?
Searching for a life
Outside of mayhem

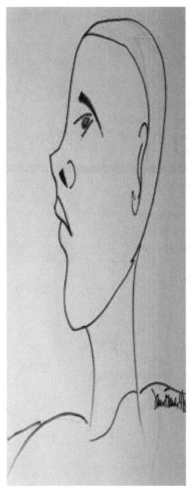

I am a Refugee

I am a refugee
From Sudan
I ran from slavery
Persecution and war
I ended up in Israel

Israel put me
In a refugee camp
Hundreds of us
To one doctor
For weeks
No shower

I was stuck in limbo
With nothing to do
Thinking day and night
Of peace and liberty
I see no solidarity
No humanity
Only more repression
And inhumanity

I am a Refugee

I am a refugee
One of several
 Millions
Families with children
Our men were killed
Only widows are left
With the burden
To feed and raise
Our children

We live in tents
In the wilderness
In harsh winters
Unbearably long hot
Scotching summers

Is war a way?
To fix the world?
What is the use of fighting?
If we'll be all dead
Or psychologically ruined
When it is done

I Am a Victim

I am a woman
I am a victim
Of colonialism
Racist history
White supremacy
And male egotism

I am a victim of
Subjugation
Oppression
Social
Demoralization
And patriarchal
 Supremacy
I am not inferior to a man
Neither am I weaker

In a dubious plot
Patriarchy placed itself
In a superior position
To matriarchy

When a woman act
Forthrightly
Men have said
She thinks like a man
Some have said the absurd
A woman's place
 Is in the kitchen

A woman's place
Is where she chooses
Home, office, space
Or on the high seas

Because she's a woman
Prejudices are vented
Against her opinions
It is a woman's freedom
To talk
She should
 Whenever she must

If biblical stereotypes
Are used to judge a woman
That woman is a victim
Of God 's unbalanced
Creation
Man in his image
Woman from man's rib
To serve God and man
What was God up to?

If a man uses Eve's character
As a model of expectations
Of his woman
She is a victim
Of his unjustness

Biblical Eve
Is a woman model
For white supremacy
And to shame
And oppress women

Fictional Eve
Is a victim of Gods
Unjustness
God punished her
For expressing
Her rights
And sexual freedoms

Eve received the greater
Punishment
For a mistake
Adam equally made

It is a plot
Eve is created
Like that

All women are victims
Of God's unjustness
And man's reckless
Willful oppression
Women are branded
And judged
 By biblical stereotypes

Don't judge me
By what biblical
Chauvinists
Say of women

I am not like "dough"
I am not a "broad"
Or "witch"
If I break loose
It is to express myself

I am not
A "piece of tail"
"Beginning of sin"
Or" the cause
Of humanities
Endless suffering"

I am not a "donkey"
" Enemy of faith"
Or "gateway to hell"

385

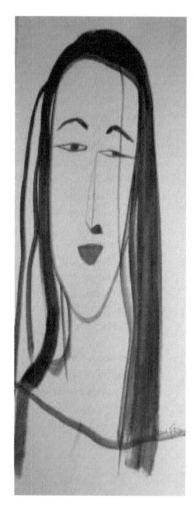

"Small as an ant"
The "greatest
 Evil Zeus made"
Or "leader of all
 Wickedness"

My "sweet-talking
And beauty"
Is not to "beguile
 A man's good sense"
To get his money

The "fascination
 Of my shape"
Is not to "overwhelm
him with charm"

I am not "overcome
 By the spirit of fornication
 More than a man
Neither are my vices
 More than a man
I am not "Narrow-minded"

Or "dark as the moon"
"Insinuating"
"indiscrete"
Or unintelligent"
"Dragon lady
"She-devil or
"Double- edge sword"
Diva? maybe

A woman should not submit
To a man
Man is not "The head of woman"
Man and woman are entitled
To equal rights
And responsibilities

A woman should not learn
In silence
With subjugation
As the bible says
Or cover her head
Nonsense!
A woman should not
Allow herself to be silenced

My aim is not
 To usurp authority
Over man
But work with him
In harmony

I maybe
"Changeable
As water"
Exceptional
Unusual
Even abnormal
Sometimes

A man
May find it
Difficult
To understand me
 I am different
From him
But not lesser

Women are
 victims

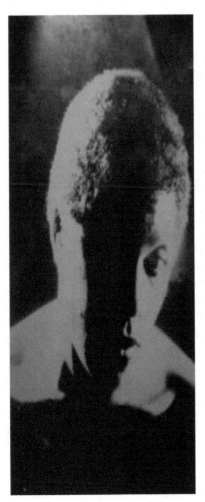

Victims of archaic laws
Biblical myths
 Sexual stereotypes
 Religious bias
 Falsified history
A one-sided masculine
Chauvinistic perspective
Of civilization

An unjust god that
Favors man over
Woman
A dubious plot
 By patriarchy
 To control the world
And dominate woman

And the fall of woman
From matriarchal supremacy
To patriarchal bondage

All women are
Victims

Women! With Raised Vices

Let your opinions
Be heard
Influence change
For a better world

I am Malala Yusuf
From Afghanistan
Taliban shot me
 In the head
On my way to school

Taliban do not want
Women to be educated
But education
 Is the only answer
For women's liberation
From ancient traditions
In Afghanistan

Tell them
Tawakkol Karman
Yemeni
Nobel Prize winner

People starving
Blockade raging
Innocent people
Stuck in the middle
No common ground
To be found

Hungry children
Fighting off death
A father not sure
He will survive
The kidney he sold
To save his family
Passes on
His responsibility
To his
Eight-year-old son

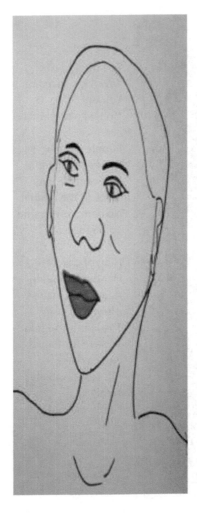

Black activist
Malkia Cyril
Antar Davidson
Malcolm Jenkins
Michael Bennett
Kevin Kaepernick
Tell the people
 What is going on?

Amie Goodman
On Democracy Now
Tell the people
What is going on

Rev William Barber
Rev Al Sharpton
One America
Two justice systems
One exclusively
 For men of color
Accused the victim
 Of being the predator

Tell the people
What is going on?

Tell the people
The world
Is losing it fast

Since women's rule
Was overthrown
Chaos keeps coming
And out of control
Only a miracle
And only women
Can save it
From total collapse

Sexual politics unfolds
Machismo power
 Crumbles
From Hollywood
 To congress
The secret thing
 Women do not
Find comfortable
 Discussing
Is unfolding
Women are telling
Of male sexual
Abusing

In politics
News media
And entertainment
Sexual exploitation
Has no end

Men with money
And power
Unable to control
Their desire
Harass women
If they could

Corporate media
On fire
Journalism reputation
In on the chopping
Block
Social media maybe
The answer

Cooperate crisis looms
Off shore secrets leak
Leakers get killed
Killers get impunity

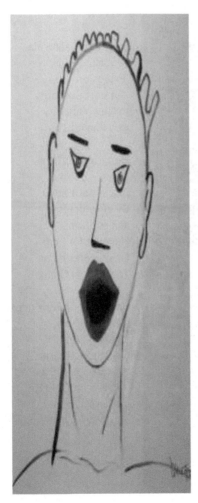

Innocent people
Peace activists
Freedom fighters
Are gunned down

The powerful
Make more weapons
Wage more wars
Kill to oppress
 Conquer
 And divide

They build
 More prisons
Defund education
Seigneur avoir mise
Cor De sur nous

Deadly virus
Genocide
Murder
Rape
Torture
 Are on the loose

Southern California
On fire
Explosion
On port authority
In New York City
Red line crossed

Hurricane Katrina
Made a point
Black, poor and
Disenfranchised
On rooftops
Flagging for help
From water rising
To swallow them

George bush flew over
Watched from
His helicopter
Ghetto in America
His mother whispered
In his ear, "They're
Underprivileged
Anyway"

Saudis Arabia
Has a new
Vision
For its nation
No 2030
Women can now
Watch
Football

Soon they may
 Be able
To watch a movie
Go to a ball game
Or join the army

They may be able
 To own a driver's
 License
Soon
The sun may shine
On their beautiful
Necklines

Will a Woman Rule the Modern World?

Will a Woman
Rule the modern
World?
Patriarchal overthrow
Looms on the horizon
Which woman
Will it be?

A world revolution
Is pending
And women
Would be leading
Which woman
Will it be?

The world is changing fast
Patriarchal rule
Is ending
A woman would be
Leading
Will women be ready?

Hilary Clinton

Hilary took a chance
 To rule
The superpower
Nation
She broke
The glass ceiling
But failed
 To go through

Some claimed
She lost the race
Because of her own
Ambitious games

But it will take
A David and Goliath game
To undo
The sharp broken glass
Stuck in the ceiling's frame
Before a woman
 Can pass through

She did well, however
Attempting to climb
The patriarchal tower

Jill stein
Saw
A light
Social
Justice
Feminist
Fighting
For earth
Peace
People
Planet
And human
Rights

Rocks and eggs
From the far left
Hit *Marie le pen*
In the head

She used
Fascists
Islamophobic
Far-right
Tactics
Against hungry
Immigrants
And systems
Helping them

She got
What she got
Must hope
For the best
The way
She chose
To help France
Was the way
To lose

Su Jun Park

Su Jun Park
Of South Korea
Walked
Led away
In handcuffs
Impeached
For corruption

Delmar Yusuf

Delmar Yusuf
Of Brazil
Another
Heroine
In peril

Impeached
For
Corruption
Is this
Another
Patriarchal
Scandal

403

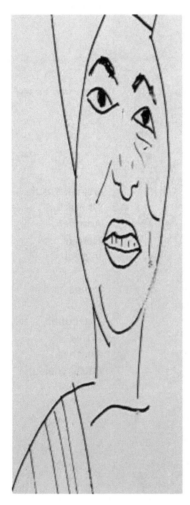

Ellen Johnson

Stepped down
Liberia's Nobel
Laureate
President
For Six years
First female
Democratically
Elected leader
Anywhere
In Africa

She brought
Stability
To a country
Torn by conflicts
Ebola
And mass
Poverty

Leymah Roberta Gbowee

Role model
Peace activist
Led
 A
 movement
To end
 Liberia's
 Civil war

More
 Women
 In power
 In Rwanda
 Malawi
And
 Gambia

Catherine Samba

International
Criminal
Court
Judge
Catherine
Samba
Jailed
Charles
 Taylor
Ellen's
 Predecessor

She jailed him
Fifty years
For crimes
In Liberia's
 Civil war
And crimes
 Against
 Humanity

Theresa May!

Pleaded a deserter
You take away
A man's wife
You take away
His soul
You leave him
With a broken
 Heart
And a child
To raise alone

If my wife crosses
The border
She will be arrested
For deserting a war
The world detested

Theresa May!
What do you say?
You pulled Britain
 Out of BREXIT
And left the union
Crumbling

You borrowed
 A phrase or two
From the labor party
In a disappointed
Election
Didn't know what to do

You vowed to stay
If the party let her play
Some feel
She should go away

You cried in dismay
Freedom democracy
 Human rights
You looked at symptoms
Not causes for solutions

Ms. May
 Don't throw stones
At glass windows
Perhaps London wars
 In foreign lands
Caused much
Of England's confusion

Angela Markel

Dear Ms. Markel
You are a champion
A true humanitarian
With a good heart
I love you so much
 For that

I saw you
 In your pink jacket
At the 20G summit
I wondered how you felt
The only woman
Surrounded
 By some
Patriarchal hawks
I wondered
If they gave you
Equal time
In the conversations

It takes a woman
Like you
With vision
And compassion
To get women
Out of silent complicity
And subjugation

Things cannot
 Go the same
 Ms. Merkle
Only a woman
Can change the game
Patriarchy only sees
Wars and inequality
A world revolution
 Is pending
And women
Would be leading

Suffer not a woman
On your mission
Let them say
Great things happened
On Ms. Merkle's watch

Aung San Suu Kyi

You find yourself
In cattle belly
Crossway
The Rhuinga
Is your nemesis
The Rhuinga
Is the magic
That will prove
You are worth it
Stand up!
Do the right thing
As the world
Watches

The world
Is changing
Patriarchal rule
Is crumbling
Take a stand
Carve a new vision

Kamala Harris

Kamala walked through
The glass ceiling
Hilary broke
To face patriarchal wrath
In a structure designed
Against women
Especially women
like her

Patriarchy, afraid
Of what women can do
Keep democracy
Unbalanced
Without matriarchal
Contributions

If Kamala fights a good fight
She might get
To where no woman
Has ever been before
It takes women like her
To change
The patriarchal view

AOC

Woman of power
Sits Shoulder
To shoulder
Holding
Her ground
Among men
Programmed
To control
The crown

She has vision
That can change
The nation
She must raise
Her voice louder
Must keep her Eyes
On the Prize
Sexism
Will press
Harder
As she climbs
Higher

Stacy's Abrams
Stacy's heart beats
 For Georgia
Sweet Georgia
Fighting
 To secure
 The vote
For Black and
Disenfranchised
People

She's a woman
Of substance
A woman of power
With integrity
With vision
 On a mission
To secure the people's
Right to vote
 She's a movement
For a new view
Of humanity
A chance to turn
 Things around
For all humanity

414

Ilhan Omar

Woman of power
Fights a good fight
Makes good trouble
To overcome
The evils of
 Racism
 Sexism
 Bigotry
 And patriarchal
 Superiority

The evils of religion
Is a factor
In any vision
To fix humanity
Tradition is a factor
In the unending struggle
For women's liberty
Tradition is a factor
In the evils
Plaguing
Humanity

415

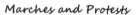

Marches and Protests

Tell the people
About the outrage
Demonstrations
Riots, boycotts
Sit-ins, strikes
Civil disobedience
Violent and non-violent
Resistance
Marches and protests
Going on
In every nation

People march
And protest
About the way
The world is run
About greedy
Corporations
Guaranteeing profits
For themselves
Don't care a hoot
About anyone else

People march
 By millions
 By thousands
One Million Men
One Million women
For life
 liberty
 Security
Equality
Opportunity

They march for
Peace
 Earth
Science
Animal rights
Human rights
Rain forests
Climate justice

They march against
 Global warming
They march to save earth
 From extinction

In America
Open carry is a
Constitutional right
Ten billion people
Ten billion guns
Student march
For safer schools
And gun laws

Teacher march
For higher wages
Others march against
 Low wage
 No job
 Unemployment
 High taxes
And for $15 an hour

They march against
Racism
Slavery
 Rape
Murder
And police
 Brutality

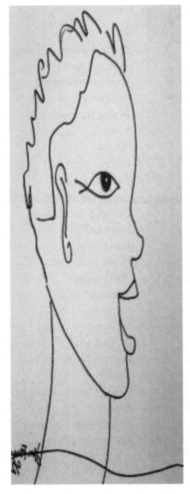

People march against
Child sex trade
And murder of children

Protests upon protests
Filled the streets
Black Lives Matter
Me Too
Shame
Violence against
 Women

Day without
 Immigrant's
Day without
 Latinos
Day of rage
Gates of hell
Pussy riot
G20 summit

Arab spring protest
Feminist protest
 In Argentina
 Protests for water
 And toilets
 In Cape Town
 South Africa

419

Standing Rock
 Dakota Access
 Pipeline protest
Indigenous protest
In Bogota Colombia
Nigerians' protests
 SARS
Farmer's protest
 In New Delhi

Cuban's protest
For food
And medicine
Israel's protest
 Netanyahu
Sudan protest
Omar Al-Bashir

Protest on holy sites
Protest for religious
 Freedom
Great March of Return
Protest
Palestinian's protest
For return to Gaza

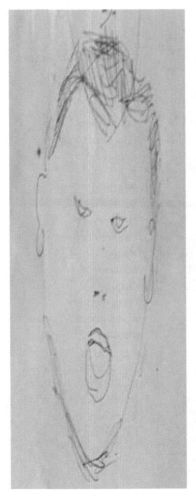

Protests against
Fascism In Rome
Trump travel ban
And anti-Asian protest
In America
Anti-coup protests
In Myanmar
Anti-corruption protest
In Guatemala

Anti-lockdown
Anti-racism
Anti-Colonialist
Pro and anti-
Government protests
In France
And other countries

Neo Nazi on the rise
Protest
White supremist
Insurrection
On the US capital
Pro-Democracy
In Hon Kong
Thailand
And Myanmar

Crime bill in UK protest
Authoritarianism
Imperialism
Capitalism
Colonialism
Fiscal austerity
Everywhere

Peaceful
Sit down
Lie down
Chained up
Naked
Solitary
Occupy
Hunger strike
And Violent
 Protests

The world Is restless
Unending upheavals
Democracy is on trial
Wars and hunger
Capitalism is the winner

Mass mobilizing
For better living
Peace and security
The working-class
 Is dissatisfied
The poor get poorer
The rich richer

It's happening
In one form
Or another
In countries
Big and small
Rich and poor
New and old

In Europe
 France
Germany
London
Poland
Norway
Sweden

In all fifty
United States
Of rich America

In India
Pakistan
Myanmar
Bangladesh
North Korea
North, South, East
And West Africa
Latin America
Australia

Belarus
Maldives
Ukraine
Bosnia
Serbia
Srebrenica
Catalonia
Philippines
Columbia

Bolivia
Brazil
French Guiana
Venezuela
Egypt
Ethiopia

Eritrea
Uganda
South Sudan
China
Canada
Congo

Johannesburg
Jamaica
Japan
Iraq
Iran
Algeria
Angola
Lebanon
Palestine

Morocco
Turkey
Syria
Saudi Arabia
Libya
Tunisia
Afghanistan
Albania

425

426

Made in the USA
Columbia, SC
05 June 2022

61346332R00241